MW01076754

BOOK OF MORMON

STORIES *for* KIDS

VOLUME ONE • FIRST NEPHI—MOSIAH

This book belongs to:

_____

BOOK OF MORMON

STORIES *for* KIDS

VOLUME ONE • FIRST NEPHI—MOSIAH

Text adapted by Jason Zippro
Illustrated by Alycia Pace

ISBN 13: 978-1-7349053-2-8

REL046000 RELIGION / Christianity / Church of Jesus Christ of Latter-day Saints (Mormon)
REL091000 RELIGION / Christian Education / Children & Youth
JNF049200 JUVENILE NONFICTION / Religious / Christian / Early Readers

Cover design © 2021 Primary Scriptures, LLC
Illustrations by Alycia Pace
Cover design by Angela Baxter
Edited and typeset by Emily Chambers and Kaitlin Barwick

Distributed by

CEDAR FORT
Publishing & Media

10 9 8 7 6 5 4 3

www.PrimaryScriptures.com

CONTENTS

CONTENTS

Mosiah   239

CONTENTS

THE FIRST
BOOK OF NEPHI

Lehi Sees a Vision of the Savior

1 NEPHI 1

Lehi was a prophet of God. He and his family lived in the city Jerusalem.

One day, Lehi prayed for the people of his city. While he prayed, a pillar of fire came down on a rock in front of him. God showed him many things in the fire. The things Lehi saw made him shake.

Lehi grew very tired, so he returned home and fell asleep on his bed. While he slept, God showed Lehi more things in a vision. Lehi saw God sitting on His throne.

Lehi saw many angels singing about God. He watched as one angel, followed by twelve other angels, came and handed him a book to read.

Lehi read the book and felt the Spirit of God. Lehi shouted, "God and the things that He does are wonderful! God will help all His children!"

Lehi's Family Leaves Jerusalem

1 NEPHI 2

One night, God spoke to Lehi in a dream. God said, "You are blessed, Lehi, because you have obeyed me. Now, I have another commandment for you: You must take your family and go far away from Jerusalem."

When Lehi woke up, he obeyed God. Lehi and his family packed up many of their things. Then they left their home in Jerusalem.

After many days they set up their tents by a river near the Red Sea. Lehi took some stones and built an altar. Lehi prayed at the altar to thank God for their safety.

Nephi Is Blessed by God

1 NEPHI 2

Lehi had four sons: Laman, Lemuel, Sam, and Nephi. His youngest son, Nephi, was strong and loved God.

Nephi prayed to God. He wanted to know if all the things his father saw in his visions and dreams were true. God sent the Spirit to help Nephi know. The Spirit gave Nephi a warm feeling in his heart that meant the visions and dreams were true.

Nephi told his brothers what God had helped him learn. Sam believed what Nephi taught, but Laman and Lemuel did not believe Nephi.

Nephi prayed for Laman and Lemuel. After Nephi prayed, God said, "Nephi, you are blessed because you have faith and believe in me. If you keep my commandments, I will lead you to a promised land."

Nephi Is Obedient

1 NEPHI 3

Lehi had another dream. In this dream, God told Lehi to send his sons back to Jerusalem. They needed to get a special book of scripture called the Plates of Brass.

When Lehi told Laman and Lemuel what God had asked, they complained and whined. They did not want to go.

When Lehi told Nephi what God had asked, Nephi showed faith. Nephi said, "I will do what God has commanded. I know God won't command us to do something, unless He helps us do what He commanded."

After Nephi said this to his father, Lehi was very happy. Lehi knew that God had blessed Nephi.

Laban Keeps the Plates of Brass
1 NEPHI 3

Nephi and his brothers went back to Jerusalem for the Plates of Brass. They sent Nephi's older brother Laman to ask for the Plates of Brass from a wicked man named Laban. Laban did not like Laman. Laban called him a thief and sent him away.

Nephi and his brothers were sad Laman didn't get the plates. Nephi said, "We will not go back to our father Lehi until we have done what God has commanded. Let's go to our old home and get all our gold, silver, and expensive things. We can use them to buy the Plates of Brass from Laban."

So Nephi and his brothers brought their gold, silver, and expensive things to Laban. When Laban saw their riches, he became very greedy. Laban sent his servants after Nephi and his brothers to kill them.

Nephi and his brothers had to run away to save their lives. They had to leave all their gold, silver, and expensive things behind, so they could escape.

Laman and Lemuel were very angry with Nephi because they lost all their things. They were so angry that they got a pole and began hitting Sam and Nephi with it.

Then an angel came and stopped Laman and Lemuel from hitting Sam and Nephi. The angel asked, "Why do you hit your younger brothers with a pole? Don't you know that God has chosen Nephi to be your leader because you do not obey God's commandments? Go back to Jerusalem and God will help you with Laban."

Nephi Gets the Plates of Brass

1 NEPHI 4

Nephi said to his brothers, "Let's go back to Jerusalem and obey God's commandments. God is stronger than the whole earth, so He is stronger than all of Laban's servants. Don't you believe that we can get the Plates of Brass from Laban with God's help?"

Laman and Lemuel were still angry with Nephi, but they followed Nephi back to Jerusalem. Nephi had his brothers wait outside the city, while he snuck in at night.

Nephi didn't know what he needed to do. He followed the feelings of the Spirit. As Nephi got closer to Laban's house, he found Laban lying on the ground, motionless.

Nephi took Laban's sword and looked at how beautiful and well made it was. Then the Spirit told Nephi to kill Laban. Nephi didn't want to because he knew that God had commanded that we should not kill.

But the Spirit told Nephi again that God needed Nephi to kill Laban. The Spirit said Nephi's family needed the Plates of Brass. The plates had all the scriptures and commandments of God written in them.

Nephi obeyed. Then Nephi put on Laban's clothes and went to Laban's servant named Zoram. Nephi pretended to be Laban. He told Zoram to bring him the Plates of Brass and come with him.

Nephi led Zoram outside the city to Nephi's brothers. Nephi showed Zoram he wasn't Laban. He made Zoram promise to leave Jerusalem with them. So Zoram, Nephi, and his brothers journeyed back to Lehi and Sariah with the Plates of Brass.

Sariah and the Return of Her Sons
1 NEPHI 5

While Nephi and his brothers were away, their mother Sariah thought they had died. Sariah complained to Lehi, "You are a dreamer! You made us leave our home and brought us to the desert. My sons are gone, and we will die here in the desert too!"

Lehi tried to comfort her, "I know I see visions. Without my visions, I would not have known to leave Jerusalem. We would be destroyed like everyone else. Now, I know that God will protect our sons from Laban. God will bring our sons back to us."

When Nephi and his brothers returned, Sariah was very happy. She said, "Now I know God has commanded my husband Lehi to come to the desert. I know that God protected my sons!"

Lehi was so happy that he offered a sacrifice and
a burnt offering to thank God. Then Lehi began to
read the Plates of Brass. He wanted to know more
about his ancestors and learn from the scriptures.

Ishmael and His Family Join Lehi

1 NEPHI 7

God commanded Lehi to send his sons to Jerusalem again. They needed to bring a man named Ishmael and his family back to the desert. So Nephi and his brothers went to get Ishmael and his family.

Ishmael obeyed God's commandment to go with Lehi's family. Ishmael's family took their things and left Jerusalem.

Laman, Lemuel, and some of Ishmael's children did not want to leave Jerusalem. They got angry with Nephi for making them leave.

Nephi said, "Laman and Lemuel, you are my older brothers. Why do I always have to be the good example for you? Don't you remember you've seen an angel? That God saved us from Laban and helped us get the Plates of Brass?"

Nephi's words made Laman and Lemuel very angry. They tied Nephi up and left him so wild animals could eat him. Nephi prayed for strength to escape. God answered his prayer.

When Laman and Lemuel saw that Nephi had escaped, they got even angrier. Ishmael's wife and children talked to Laman and Lemuel until they felt bad for tying Nephi up.

Laman and Lemuel asked Nephi to forgive them. Nephi quickly forgave them and told them they should pray and ask God to forgive them too. After Laman and Lemuel prayed, they all journeyed back to Lehi and Sariah.

Lehi's Vision of the Tree of Life

1 NEPHI 8

One night, Lehi had another dream. In the dream, Lehi saw a tree. The tree was covered in special, white fruit. Lehi ate some of the fruit, which was sweet and filled him with joy.

Lehi wanted his family to have some so they could feel the joy he felt. As he looked for them, he saw a river next to the tree. He looked far up the river until he saw his wife Sariah and two of his sons, Sam and Nephi.

He called to them. They came and ate some of the
white fruit. Then Lehi saw Laman and Lemuel, but
when he called to them, they did not want to come.

Lehi noticed that along the edge of the river was a small path. Along the path was an iron rod for people to hold on to. He also saw that the path and iron rod went all the way back past the beginning of the river into a very large field.

Lehi saw that the field was full of people. Some people began to follow the path toward the tree.

Soon a dark fog covered the field and path. Some of the people couldn't find their way anymore and got lost in the darkness.

Others grabbed the iron rod and followed it until they got to the tree and ate the fruit.

Across the river from the tree was a very large building. There were all kinds of people in it dressed in fancy clothes.

The people in the building were pointing at the people eating the white fruit of the tree. They were making fun of those eating the fruit and laughing at them.

Some of the people eating the fruit felt bad that the people in the building were laughing at them. They stopped eating the fruit and walked off into the dark fog and got lost.

But many of the people eating the fruit ignored the people in the building making fun of them. These people felt happy eating the fruit.

There were many people who went into the building. Others slipped and fell into the river. Others got lost in the darkness.

When Lehi woke from his dream, he told his family what he had seen. He was happy that Sam and Nephi listened and came to eat the fruit. He was sad and worried for Laman and Lemuel because they did not want to come.

Lehi's Testimony

1 NEPHI 10

Lehi shared his testimony with his family. Lehi said, "In 600 years, God will send a prophet to the Jews. This prophet will be Jesus Christ, the Savior of the world.

Another prophet will come before Jesus Christ. This prophet will preach to the people to prepare themselves for Christ's coming. His name will be John the Baptist.

John will baptize Jesus Christ and many other people. John will say he has baptized the Lamb of God, who will take away the sins of the world."

Lehi taught his children that the Jews won't believe Jesus. They will kill him. But after Jesus dies, He will return. He'll show Himself to people that aren't Jews, called Gentiles.

And Lehi shared many more things in his testimony to his family about Jesus Christ.

Nephi Has a Vision

1 NEPHI 11–12

Nephi was thinking deeply about Lehi's visions, when Nephi had a vision of his own. In the vision, Nephi was standing on the top of a mountain. The Spirit asked him, "What do you want?" Nephi said, "I want to see the things my father Lehi saw in his visions."

The Spirit asked, "Do you believe your father saw the tree with white fruit?" And Nephi said, "I believe everything my father has seen."

The Spirit shouted, "Hooray! Because you believe in God, you are blessed, Nephi. Now look!" Nephi looked and saw the tree with the white fruit. "What does it mean?" asked Nephi.

The Spirit showed Nephi the city of Nazareth. In the city there was a beautiful woman. The woman gave birth to a baby boy—Jesus Christ.

The Spirit also showed Nephi Jesus as an adult teaching many people.

The Spirit explained, "The iron rod is the word of God, which will always lead you to the tree. The tree is the Love of God."

The Spirit showed Nephi the baptism of Jesus, the Twelve Apostles of Jesus, and the death of Jesus.

Nephi then saw the building full of people from Lehi's vision. He saw it get destroyed. "The building is the pride of the world, and everyone who fights against God will be destroyed."

"Look!" the Spirit told Nephi. Nephi saw the promised land. There were many people angry with each other. The people battled against each other.

Then dark fog covered the land. There were earthquakes. There was lightning and fire. There were people scared and crying. The Spirit said, "the dark fog is the temptations of Satan. It confuses you to not believe in God."

Then Nephi saw the dark fog disappear. Jesus Christ came down from heaven and showed Himself to the people. Then the Spirit showed Nephi many more things that would happen in the promised land and the world.

The Liahona
1 NEPHI 16

While living by the Red Sea, Lehi had another dream. God told Lehi to keep traveling away from Jerusalem.

In the morning, Lehi went to leave his tent. By the door, he found an interesting brass ball.

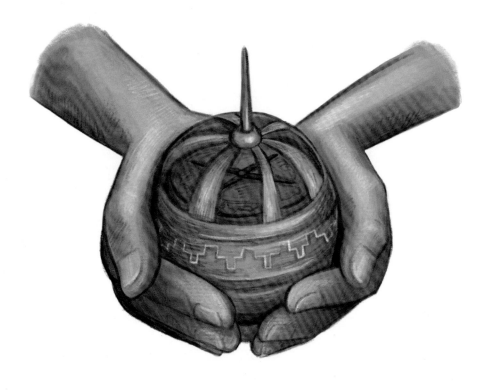

Inside of the brass ball were two little pointers. They showed Lehi the direction he needed to go. The brass ball was called the Liahona.

So Lehi obeyed God's commandment. Lehi, Ishmael, and their families gathered their things and began traveling again.

Nephi Breaks His Bow

1 NEPHI 16

Lehi followed the directions of the Liahona. The Liahona helped the families find their way to places where there was food and water.

After many days of traveling, the families stopped to rest for a while. Nephi took his steel bow and went to hunt for food. While Nephi was hunting, his bow broke.

His brothers were angry because they couldn't get any food without Nephi's bow. Everyone complained and whined because they were so hungry, even Lehi.

Nephi did not complain. Instead, Nephi decided to
make a new bow and some arrows from wood.

When Nephi finished, he asked Lehi where to go hunt for food. Lehi prayed. God told Lehi that he should not have complained. Lehi felt sorry. Nephi followed the Liahona's directions for where to find food.

Nephi learned the Liahona only worked if everyone had faith and followed God's commandments written in it. He learned that God can use little things, like the Liahona, to make big and important things happen.

Arrival to the Land Bountiful

1 NEPHI 17

Nephi's family traveled for many years. They followed the Liahona and obeyed God's commandments from the Liahona.

Many things happened while they traveled. Ishmael grew old and died. Lehi and Sariah had two more sons, Jacob and Joseph. The families had many struggles. God always blessed them when they obeyed His commandments.

After eight years, the family arrived at a beautiful place by the ocean. This place was full of fruit, honey, and fresh water. The family stayed here and called the place Bountiful.

Nephi Builds a Ship

1 NEPHI 17

One day, God told Nephi to go up the nearby mountain. When Nephi got to the top of the mountain, he prayed to God. God commanded Nephi to build a ship. God showed Nephi how to build it.

God said the ship would take Nephi and his family across the ocean to a promised land. "I will be your light. I will guide you if you keep my commandments. When you arrive, you will know that I am God and that I have led you from Jerusalem to this new land."

So Nephi began to build the ship. As Nephi worked, Laman and Lemuel began to complain. They did not want to help build. They made fun of Nephi, saying that he was silly to think he could build a ship. They did not believe God had showed Nephi how to build a ship.

This made Nephi very sad. Nephi said to his brothers, "Don't you remember the story of Moses and how God helped His people to escape Egypt? God parted the Red Sea so they could escape. God also fed them with bread that fell from the sky and gave them water to drink from a rock!

God helped Moses and his people, like God helped our family escape from Jerusalem. You have been disobedient even though you have seen an angel. I am afraid that you will be destroyed because of the way you have both behaved."

When Laman and Lemuel heard what Nephi had said, they were angry and wanted to throw him in the ocean. They tried to grab Nephi.

Nephi said, "In the name of God, do not touch me! If you do, God will destroy you. Stop your complaining and help me build this ship. God commanded me to build it, and I will obey Him. I can do anything that God tells me to do."

God told Nephi to touch Lamen and Lemuel. Nephi did, and God shocked them. Laman and Lemuel believed and began to help Nephi build the ship.

Nephi Is Tied to the Ship

1 NEPHI 18

Nephi finished building the ship. Everyone helped fill the ship with food, water, and things they would need. Then they set off for the promised land.

Laman, Lemuel, the sons of Ishmael, and their wives began to behave badly. They said very rude things. Nephi worried God would get angry, so Nephi told them to stop.

Laman and Lemuel were angry, "We will not let our younger brother be our leader." They took Nephi and tied him up.

As soon as they tied up Nephi, the Liahona stopped working. They didn't know where to steer the ship. Soon a great storm rocked the ship back and forth. They left Nephi tied to the ship for four days. The storm got worse and worse. They thought the ship would sink into the sea.

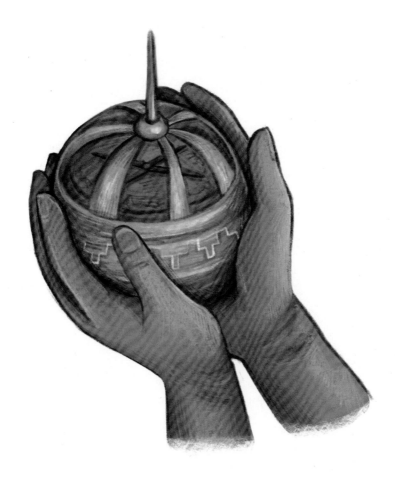

Laman and Lemuel were so afraid that they finally let Nephi go. Nephi's ankles and wrists were swollen, but Nephi did not complain. Nephi picked up the Liahona, and it began to work again.

Nephi prayed to God. The storm stopped, and the ocean was calm again. Nephi guided the ship for many days. Nephi and the families finally arrived in the promised land.

The Small and Large Plates of Nephi
1 NEPHI 9 & 19

God told Nephi to make a record. Nephi obeyed by making two sets of metal books called plates. He made a large set of plates and a small set of plates.

On the large plates, Nephi wrote down everything that happened to his family. He wrote about their journey from Jerusalem to the promised land.

On the small plates, Nephi wrote down spiritual things to help his people remember Jesus Christ.

Nephi Teaches His Brothers

1 NEPHI 20–22

Nephi wanted his brothers to always remember Jesus Christ. So, Nephi read from the scriptures to teach them. Nephi read the words of a prophet named Isaiah.

Nephi's brothers did not understand Isaiah. They asked Nephi to tell them what Isaiah's words meant. Nephi explained that God's people, the House of Israel, will spread out over the whole earth.

After Israel has spread out, God will create a great
country. This country will be full of people, called
Gentiles, who are not from the House of Israel.

In this great country, God will share His covenants and gospel with the people. God will then bring the House of Israel back to their homeland, and they will know Jesus Christ.

God will call a prophet and command us to listen and obey his words. Nephi told his brothers, "if we continue to obey God's commandments until the end of our lives, we will be saved."

THE SECOND BOOK OF NEPHI

Lehi Teaches Jacob about Agency

2 NEPHI 2

Lehi grew old. He wanted to share his testimony with his children. He spoke to Jacob first. "Jacob, you are blessed because you have seen God's glory!"

In this life, everything has an opposite. There is good and evil, happiness and sadness. Some things can act, and other things are there to be acted on.

Without opposites, nothing would exist. But there is a God, and He created everything. God made us so we could choose and act for ourselves between opposites.

God even created Adam and Eve and the Garden of Eden. Adam and Eve had two opposite trees: the tree with the forbidden fruit and the tree of life.

Satan wants all of us to feel unhappy. He lied to Eve and told her to eat the forbidden fruit. After Adam and Eve ate the fruit, they had to leave the Garden of Eden. This was called the Fall.

Because of the Fall, Adam and Eve could have children. They could also now choose between good and evil. They could now feel happiness and sadness. Because of their choice, we all came to earth and will die someday.

Because of the Fall, we can all choose to be good or evil. If we choose good, we can live with Heavenly Father in heaven. If we choose evil, we will be unhappy and have to live with Satan.

Lehi finished his testimony by saying, "Remember to follow Jesus Christ and His commandments. Obey His words and listen to the Holy Ghost, so you can live with God in heaven forever!"

Lehi Teaches Joseph about His Name

2 NEPHI 3

Lehi also shared his testimony with his son Joseph and blessed him. Lehi said, "You are little, Joseph, but listen to your brother Nephi, and God will bless you.

Remember that we named you after one of our ancestors, Joseph of Egypt. Joseph saw visions of us and of the future. God promised Joseph that one of his grandchildren would be a mighty prophet like Moses.

This prophet will turn our records into a book of scripture. This prophet's name is also Joseph. Joseph Smith will take the book of scripture, which is the Book of Mormon, and teach from it.

God will also turn the Jewish records into a book of scripture called The Holy Bible. Both of these scriptures will teach people the truth. They will teach about God's covenants. They will help all people believe in Jesus Christ."

Lehi Blesses His Grandchildren and Dies

2 NEPHI 4

Lehi also blessed Laman and Lemuel's children. "I give you my blessing. If you keep God's commandments, He will bless you in the promised land. God will be kind to you and not let you be completely destroyed."

Then Lehi called Sam and blessed him. "Sam, you will do well in the promised land like your brother Nephi. God will bless your children like Nephi's children."

After Lehi gave his blessings, he grew older and died. After his father died, Nephi thought about his own life. Nephi was worried because of his sins. But Nephi loved God and was grateful to Him. Nephi trusted that God would help him be better.

Nephites Separate from Lamanites

2 NEPHI 5

After Lehi died, Laman and Lemuel grew more and more angry with Nephi. They didn't like their younger brother being their leader. They grew so angry that they decided to kill Nephi. They wanted to be the leaders.

God told Nephi to travel far away from Laman and Lemuel. So Nephi took everyone who would go with him. Zoram, Sam, Jacob, Joseph, and everyone else who believed in God left with Nephi. Nephi also took the Plates of Brass, Laban's sword, and the Liahona.

Everyone who left with Nephi called themselves Nephites. Everyone who stayed with Laman and Lemuel called themselves Lamanites.

The Nephites travelled for many days. When they stopped, they started to build a new city. They built farms, buildings, and even a temple. They worked hard. They learned to make things from wood and different metals.

Nephi worried the Lamanites would come attack the Nephites. So Nephi took the sword of Laban and made many swords like it. The Nephites could use the swords to protect themselves.

God warned Nephi. The Nephites should remember God and obey His commandments. If they didn't, God would let the Lamanites destroy them.

Nephi listened to God's warning and called Jacob and Joseph to be priests. Nephi told his younger brothers to teach the Nephites. So Jacob and Joseph taught the Nephites to remember God and obey His commandments. The Nephites listened and became a very happy people.

Jacob and the Gospel

2 NEPHI 9

As a priest, Jacob went around teaching the Nephites about God and Jesus Christ. Jacob taught the Nephites why Jesus Christ is so important to God's plan.

Jacob explained that everyone on earth makes mistakes. Sometimes we choose not to follow God's commandments. When we do things God doesn't want us to, it is called sin. We sin when we disobey His commandments.

Everyone sins sometimes. When we sin, it makes our spirits unclean. Only clean spirits can live with God. When we sin, we cannot go back to live with God without help.

Jesus Christ can help us be clean from sin. He is the only person who has never sinned. He helps us fix our mistakes when we sin, so we can return to live with God.

That is why Jesus Christ came to live on earth. He came to help us be clean from sin and to help us live with God again after we die. He can do these things because of the Atonement.

Christ suffered pain in the Garden of Gethsemane.
His suffering for our sins is called the Atonement.

Christ was also hurt and died on the Cross of Calvary. But He came back to life. Because Christ died and came back to life, we can too.

When people die, their bodies and spirits separate. Resurrection is when a person's body and spirit come back together. Jesus Christ was the first person to be resurrected.

Jesus wants us to obey His commandments. Faith is when we trust Him enough to obey Him. He wants us to repent. Repenting means trying to fix our mistakes and do better next time. We also need to be baptized. Baptism is how we promise God that we will follow Him.

If we obey His commandments, have faith in Him, repent of our sins, and are baptized, then God will give us the gift of the Holy Ghost. The Holy Ghost will help us make good decisions. If we continue to obey His commandments for the rest of our lives we will return to live with God after we die.

Nephi Writes the Words of Isaiah

2 NEPHI 11

Nephi wrote in the small plates, "I have seen Christ and I love teaching my children that Christ will come again! Isaiah has also seen Christ, so I will write some of Isaiah's words."

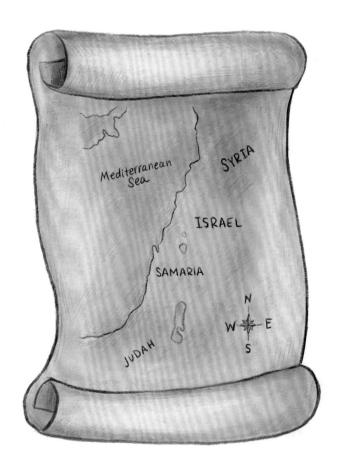

In Isaiah's day, there were many of God's people. Some lived in Jerusalem like Isaiah. They were called the people of Judah, or the Jews. Others lived in Samaria. They were called the people of Ephraim, or the Israelites.

In those days, God's people fought against each other. The Israelites fought the Jews. The Israelites brought another people, called the Syrians, to help them attack the Jews.

Isaiah Is Called as a Prophet

2 NEPHI 16

Isaiah was called to be a prophet. He had a vision where he saw God on a throne in the temple full of smoke. Angels stood by God. These angels had six wings. The wings meant they were very powerful. The angels glowed like they were on fire.

The angels shouted "Holy, holy, holy the God of Hosts, His light fills all the earth." Isaiah felt like he didn't belong because he wasn't perfect. But an angel put a hot coal on Isaiah's lips. This meant Isaiah's sins were forgiven.

God asked, "Who should I send to preach to the people?" Isaiah said, "Send me!" God warned Isaiah that many people wouldn't believe what he taught, even though Isaiah was a prophet.

Isaiah taught the people that there would be many wars because they weren't obeying God. He warned the people of Jerusalem that all God's people would be destroyed or taken as slaves.

The war between God's people in Isaiah's day is like the war between good and evil today. Isaiah wrote his words down to help us not be destroyed like his people were.

Isaiah Warns the People
for Being Wicked

2 NEPHI 12, 13, 15 & 20

Isaiah tried to warn the people about sin. He said that God's people, the House of Israel, were very wicked. They only cared about their money and things, instead of God.

Isaiah warned about Satan. Satan is trying to destroy our families. He wants children to not listen to their parents. Satan wants the women of the church to only care about what they wear and how they look. But if they do, they will only feel lonely, embarrassed, and ashamed.

Isaiah told the people that God was unhappy with them. The people didn't take care of the poor and needy. Isaiah warned that anyone who doesn't help the poor and needy, won't get help or protection when they need it. God is like a rock that protects the righteous. But the wicked will trip over the rock.

Isaiah also told the people to watch out and be careful. There are people who will try to confuse you, even in the church. They try to make you think that bad is good, that darkness is light, and that bitter is sweet. These people help the guilty and punish the innocent.

Isaiah taught that Christ is the Bread of Life and the Living Water. If the members of the church aren't following Christ, their spirits will be hungry. Remember, when we don't obey God, we sin. Sinners are like an ox pulling a cart. Sins are heavy to carry.

God's People Will Be Destroyed and Scattered

2 NEPHI 14, 15, 18

In Isaiah's time, the King of Jerusalem was called Ahaz. Isaiah revealed to King Ahaz that a great enemy was coming. They were called Assyrians. They would destroy everything except Jerusalem.

Many of the men would be killed or taken as slaves. The women would be left without husbands. But God will comfort His people by giving them a temple as a safe place to go.

Isaiah told a story. "God had a growing vineyard on a hill. He protected it with a wall and a watchtower. He cleared out the rocks so the grapes could grow well.

God did everything He could to help the grapes grow. But they still grew bad grapes. So God said, "Let my vineyard be destroyed." Isaiah warned that the vineyard in this story is like the members of the church who don't repent. They are the wicked House of Israel.

Isaiah Prophesies of Christ and the Last Days

2 NEPHI 12, 17, 19, 21

Isaiah revealed more to King Ahaz. If King Ahaz obeyed God's warnings, Jerusalem's enemies would fail. As a sign that this was true, Jesus Christ would be born.

Isaiah continued, "For us this child is born. God's Son has been given to us. He will be our ruler. He will be called Wonderful Counselor, The Mighty God, The Everlasting Father, and The Prince of Peace."

Many years after Christ, Joseph Smith will live. He will have the Spirit help him. Joseph will begin to gather all of the House of Israel. Eventually, Jews and Israelites will no longer fight.

In the last days, the Temple of God will be built. Missionaries will go into the world to bring people to the temple.

When Christ comes again, there will be peace for many years. The people of the earth will take all their weapons and turn them into useful tools.

The Evil of Babylon Destroyed

2 NEPHI 23–24

There was an evil nation called Babylon. In the last days, Babylon is a symbol for evil. Isaiah taught that Zion, God's people, will gather and destroy Babylon.

God will lift a flag in the mountains to call His soldiers to battle. The soldiers are the members of His church. His soldiers will come from all over the world.

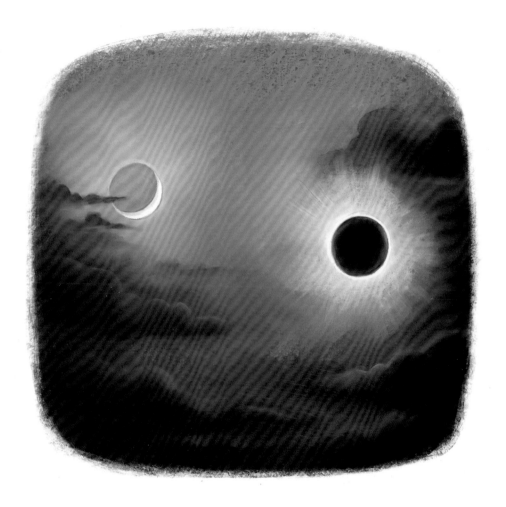

In the very last days, all people will feel afraid and guilty. The sun, moon, and stars will grow dark in the sky. The sinners will be destroyed. The earth and heaven will shake.

Once Babylon is destroyed, the survivors will be rarer than gold. Only hyenas and jackals will live in the empty, leftover buildings.

After Babylon falls, God's people will be glad. God will let them return to their own land and rest. They will say, "the whole world can now rest and be at peace. Sing for joy!"

They will also say, "Satan, who is the king of Babylon, fell from heaven. He tried to sit on God's throne, but he is now in darkness forever."

Nephi Shares His Thoughts about Isaiah's Writings

2 NEPHI 25

Nephi explained, "Isaiah's words will be important for the people in the last days. Prophets always warn the people before they are destroyed for their wickedness."

"The Jews did not listen to God, so they were destroyed. When Christ comes, the Jews will reject Him. They will crucify Him. They will put Him in a tomb. After three days though, Christ will rise from the dead."

"I have seen Christ's day! Everyone who believes in Christ will be saved in God's Kingdom. I saw that after Christ rises from the dead, Jerusalem will be destroyed again. The Jews will scatter over the whole earth."

"In the last days, God will gather His people again. He will bring them scriptures, so they will know who Jesus Christ is. I write about Christ so that my children and my people will believe in Jesus Christ. I want them to know who will forgive them of their sins."

Nephi Sees the End of His People

2 NEPHI 26

Nephi spoke more about Christ to his people. "After His resurrection, Christ will visit the Nephites to give us commandments."

Before He comes, prophets will show us signs to look for. These special signs will let us know when Christ is born. The signs will also let us know when He dies and is resurrected.

After Christ dies, there will be thunder and lightning. Many people will die in earthquakes and fire. All of the people in the promised land will suffer.

Everyone who believes the prophets will be protected. Everyone who obeys the prophets won't die. These people are called the believers. They watch for the signs even when others make fun of them.

After all the earthquakes and fires finish, Jesus Christ will come to visit. He will heal the people who are still alive. He will teach them how to have peace.

The people will become a kind and happy people for many years. The parents and children will live in peace. The grandchildren and great-grandchildren will also live in peace.

But the great-great-grandchildren will begin to not believe in Christ. They will not obey His commandments. These people will get worse and worse. They will fight each other and the Lamanites. They will fight until they are all destroyed.

Remember to follow God's commandments. Do not kill, lie, or steal. Do not swear using God's name. Do not hate someone because they have something you want. Do not hurt others or fight with each other. Do not love anything more than God.

The Gospel of Christ

2 NEPHI 32

"Remember that Jacob taught you to obey God's commandments," Nephi said. "Have faith in Jesus Christ. Repent of your sins. Be baptized. If you do these things, the Holy Ghost will help you.

The Holy Ghost speaks the words of Christ. The words of Christ tell you everything you should do. So read the scriptures because they are full of the words of Christ.

If you do not understand something, then pray to God and ask Him to help you understand. If you pray, God will help you understand by sending the Holy Ghost to teach you."

Nephi's Testimony

2 NEPHI 29–33

Nephi taught his people many things. When he was old, he shared his testimony with them. "Listen to everything I have taught you, and believe in Jesus Christ. If you don't believe in what I've taught, then at least believe in Jesus Christ.

If you believe in Jesus Christ, you will believe what I have taught you. Jesus Christ told me what to say and write, so these are His words. These words have taught you to do good.

God will show you that everything I have said are His words. He will show you that He commanded me to write them, and I obeyed Him. So listen and obey His words."

JACOB, ENOS, JAROM, OMNI, AND WORDS OF MORMON

Nephi Dies

JACOB 1

Nephi was growing too old to lead the people anymore. So, Nephi made someone king over the Nephites. The people loved Nephi because he was such a good leader. So, the people called the new king second Nephi so they would remember Nephi.

Nephi also kept the record of his people. He gave the record to Jacob. Nephi commanded Jacob to write down anything about Christ, about any visions he had, and anything that God told him to write. Jacob obeyed.

Soon, Nephi died. He had been a good ruler. He worked hard to protect his people from the Lamanites. He worked hard to help all his people be successful. He had taught them about Jesus Christ and His commandments. He taught them to obey God.

Jacob Warns of Sin

JACOB 1–3

After Nephi died, Jacob and Joseph went around and taught the Nephites to remember God. They taught the Nephites to believe in Christ and obey His commandments.

The Nephites began to sin. They didn't always obey God's commandments. They started to care more about money. They cared more about what others thought of them.

Jacob went to the temple one day to teach the people. He said, "Nephites, you are beginning to sin. God told me to talk to you. And it makes me sad that I must tell you what you are doing wrong.

Many of you are beginning to care more about money. God has been good to you and given some of you more money than others. But you think you are better than others because you have more money than they do. God does not like this.

Follow God's commandments. Use your money to help others who don't have as much as you. Give clothes to others who don't have any. Give food to others who don't have enough to eat. Help people who are in prison. Help others who are sick or sad."

The Allegory of the Olive Tree

JACOB 5

Jacob taught the people about the words of the prophet Zenos. Zenos spoke to God's people, called the House of Israel. "Pretend God's people are the branches of an old olive tree. This olive tree is in a large vineyard. Pretend the vineyard is the whole world."

God saw that His tree was beginning to get sick and die. So God tried to help the tree by giving it food and cleaning it up. When God calls a prophet, it is like feeding and cleaning up the tree. Prophets teach and warn God's people.

THE SCATTERING OF ANCIENT ISRAEL

A few good branches grew, but the tree was still sick and dying. So God cut off and burned the sick branches. The sick branches are the people who don't obey and follow God.

God then cut off the few good branches and stuck them onto wild olive trees in the vineyard. God also cut off branches from the wild olive trees and stuck them onto the old, sick, dying tree. This means God scattered His people all over the world. This is called the Scattering of Israel.

THE SCATTERING OF ANCIENT ISRAEL

Many days later, God and His servant checked on the trees. The wild olive branches made good olive fruit. The roots of the tree helped feed the branches, so they could grow healthy and strong. The roots are God's gospel and covenants. Covenants are promises we make with God.

God looked at the good branches on the wild trees. They also grew good olive fruit, even though they were planted in poor soil.

THE TIME OF CHRIST

One wild tree was growing in good soil. It's olive fruits were both good and bad. God's servant said, "don't destroy it yet. Let's clean it up and feed it, and see if it will grow good olive fruit." These branches were the Nephites and Lamanites.

Many days later, God and His servant checked on the trees again. All the olive fruit on the old tree was bad. God asked His servant, "What should we do? The roots are good. The roots don't help if the tree grows bad fruit though. And if we do nothing, the tree will die."

God went to check on the branches of the wild olive trees. All of them had also grown bad olive fruit. They checked the last tree that used to have both good and bad branches. They found that the good branch had completely died. All the Nephites and Lamanites were wicked.

God gathered the old olive tree branches that He put on the wild olive trees. He put them back onto the old olive tree. God also took the wild branches that He had put onto the old olive tree, and He put them back on the wild olive trees.

THE LATTER-DAY GATHERING OF ISRAEL

God sent His servant to get all the other servants to come work in the vineyard. It was almost time to gather the good olives. The servants needed to help clean up and feed the trees so they would grow good olives one last time. This is the prophet calling all of us to be missionaries.

The servants came and began to work. They cut off branches that were growing bad olives and burned them. With the bad branches gone, the branches growing good olives could grow better.

THE LATTER-DAY GATHERING OF ISRAEL

The servants worked long and hard. After awhile, the trees began to grow strong. They grew lots of good olives. God told His servants, "Bless you! You have listened and obeyed me. You have worked hard all this time to help the olive trees grow good olives."

"Now," said God, "when bad fruit begins to grow on the trees again, I will gather all the good fruit. I will keep the good fruit safe. Then I will burn the whole vineyard. This will happen soon."

THE LATTER-DAY GATHERING OF ISRAEL

"Remember to listen to and obey God and His servants, the prophets," Jacob explained. "We are the olives. As we obey God's commandments, we grow to be good. If we are good, God will gather and save us at the last day before He burns the rest of the world."

Sherem and Jacob

JACOB 7

Among the Nephites was a man named Sherem. Sherem started teaching the people that Jesus Christ would not come. Many people believed him because Sherem was very smart and good at speaking.

Sherem knew that Jacob believed in Christ. Sherem wanted to argue with Jacob because he wanted to make Jacob not believe in Jesus Christ. But Jacob had seen angels, and had even heard Christ speaking to him, so Sherem would not be successful.

Sherem spoke to Jacob, "You have been teaching people that Christ will someday come. You are lying because no one can know the future." Jacob replied, "Do you believe the scriptures?" Sherem said, "Yes."

Jacob replied, "All the prophets in the scriptures have written about Christ. And the Holy Ghost has told me that Christ will someday come." "If that's true," said Sherem, "then show me a sign to prove that this Holy Ghost is real."

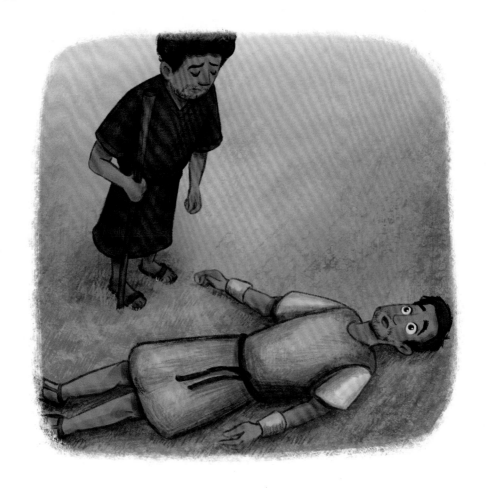

Jacob said, "If God wants to show you a sign, then let Him make you weak and fall down. But it is God's choice if He will show you a sign." Sherem immediately fell down. It took many days before he was strong enough to speak to the Nephites.

Sherem explained, "I have been tricked by Satan. Everything I have told you is a lie. Christ will come, and the Holy Ghost and angels are real. I am sad because I know God is very unhappy with what I did. I hope He forgives me." Then Sherem died.

The Nephites were amazed. They began to read the scriptures again and believe in Christ. And they began to send missionaries to teach the Lamanites about Christ.

Enos Prays to God

ENOS 1

Enos was Jacob's son. One day, Enos was in the forest hunting wild beasts, when he remembered some of his father's teachings.

Enos wanted to know if God would forgive his sins, so he knelt down and began to pray. Enos prayed all day without stopping. When night came, Enos was still praying.

While Enos was praying, God spoke to Enos. "You are blessed. Your sins are forgiven because you have faith in Jesus Christ."

When Enos heard these words, he thought about the Nephites. So Enos began to pray for the Nephites. God told Enos that if the Nephites kept God's commandments, He would visit them.

When Enos heard God's promise, he started to pray for the Lamanites. God promised Enos that God would bless the Lamanites too.

Enos learned the power of prayer. He learned that if you ask God for something good, He will give it to you, if you believe in Jesus Christ.

Jarom and Omni Pass the Records Down

JAROM & OMNI

Now the record passed down from Jacob to Enos to his son Jarom. In Jarom's days the Nephites were good. Because they kept the commandments, God blessed them to be rich and strong. God protected them from the Lamanites.

Jarom gave the records to Omni, his son. And the records got passed down again and again for over three hundred years. From Omni to Amaron. Then to Amaron's brother Chemish. Then Chemish gave them to his son Abinadom. And Abinadom gave them to his son Amaleki.

In Amaleki's days, there was a king called Mosiah. God spoke to King Mosiah and told him to take the Nephites and leave their cities. King Mosiah obeyed.

King Mosiah and the Nephites travelled far away from the land of Nephi. They came to a city called Zarahemla.

Like Lehi, the people of Zarahemla had also come from Jerusalem. God led them to the promised land too. But they had forgotten God, because they didn't have scriptures with them.

When Lehi and his family left Jerusalem, God sent Nephi and his brothers back to get the Plates of Brass. The plates had the scriptures in it so they could remember the commandments of God.

The Nephites stayed in Zarahemla. The people of Zarahemla made King Mosiah their king too. Now the people of Zarahemla and the Nephites were all called Nephites. After many years, King Mosiah's son Benjamin became King.

Amaleki, who had the records, didn't have any children to give his records to. So Amaleki gave them to King Benjamin. Benjamin was a good king who obeyed God's commandments.

The Words of Mormon

Many years after King Benjamin, there was a prophet named Mormon. In Mormon's day, all the Nephites died. They died because they no longer listened to God or obeyed His commandments.

Mormon received all the Nephite records. He had the Plates of Brass. He had the records Nephi and Jacob kept, the Small Plates of Nephi. He had the Large Plates of Nephi written by the kings of the Nephites. And he had many other records too.

God commanded Mormon to rewrite the Nephite records onto small, golden pages. These pages are the Gold Plates.

Joseph Smith was given the Gold Plates. The angel Moroni showed Joseph where to find them. Joseph translated the words from the Gold Plates. Joseph's translation is The Book of Mormon.

The Book of Mormon teaches us the great things God has done for His people. The Book of Mormon helps us remember the promises we made with God and God's commandments.

The Book of Mormon was written so all God's children would believe in Jesus Christ.

MOSIAH

Mosiah Is Chosen as King

MOSIAH 1

In the city of Zarahemla there was an old king named Benjamin. Benjamin had three sons: Mosiah, Helorum, and Helaman. King Benjamin taught them the language of their ancestors. He also wanted them to read and understand the words of the prophets.

King Benjamin taught his sons to be grateful for the records on the plates. If it weren't for the records, they wouldn't know God's commandments. The records helped them learn about and obey God.

King Benjamin grew older. He called his son Mosiah to him and said, "Mosiah, call all my people together. Tomorrow I will make you king over all the people. I will also give the people a new name because they have been good and kept the commandments of God."

King Benjamin gave Mosiah all the records. King Benjamin gave him the Plates of Brass and the small and large plates of Nephi. He also gave Mosiah the Sword of Laban and the Liahona. Then Mosiah went and told all the people to gather at the temple the next day.

King Benjamin Teaches His People

MOSIAH 2

The Nephite families came and set up their tents facing the temple. There were so many people that King Benjamin stood on a tower so the people could hear him speak. King Benjamin had scribes write down what he said so those who could not hear him could read his words.

King Benjamin spoke to his people. "I've asked you to come listen to my words and do what I will teach you. I have taught you to keep the commandments of God. And though I am your king, I have not asked you for money. I have worked with my own hands to serve you.

I don't tell you this to show you how great I am. Instead, I want you to learn that when you serve others, you are serving God. And if I, a king, am willing to serve you, shouldn't you serve each other?

If you are thankful for me, I say be even more thankful to your heavenly King! All God asks you to do is obey His commandments. Those who keep God's commandments will be blessed.

I gathered you together to tell you I can no longer be your king. I am getting old. So, I am making my son Mosiah your king. Keep the commandments God will give you through Mosiah. You will continue to be blessed.

Be careful to not get angry and argue with each other. If you do, you are choosing to follow the evil spirit. If you keep following the evil spirit, you will suffer endless punishment.

If you do not follow the truth you are taught, the Spirit of God will leave you. The Spirit cannot live in unclean places. If you do not repent, you will feel guilty. You will feel pain like a hot fire. I want you to think about how awful the disobedient feel.

Think about how blessed and happy the obedient feel. The obedient keep the commandments of God. God blesses them with spiritual and earthly things. If they keep obeying, they will live with God. They will always be happy.

King Benjamin Teaches about Jesus Christ

MOSIAH 3

I also want to teach you a few things that an angel has taught me. The angel told me to rejoice! Soon, the Savior will be born on earth and have a body. His name is Jesus Christ, the Son of God. His mother will be called Mary.

Jesus will work many miracles. He will heal the sick and raise the dead. He will help the blind to see and the deaf to hear. He will cure many people of sickness. He will cast out evil spirits.

Jesus Christ will come to earth to save all humankind, if they have faith in Him. He will suffer for everyone's wrongs and the evil they do. He will suffer such great pain that He will bleed from every pore.

But many will not believe in Him. They will hurt Him and crucify Him. After three days, He will rise from the dead. We can only be saved if we repent and have faith in Jesus Christ.

God sends prophets to teach about Jesus Christ. Prophets teach us to believe in Jesus Christ. They want us to learn how our sins can be forgiven so we can feel joy.

There will be no other person who can save us except Jesus Christ. We must believe we can only be saved by Jesus Christ. We are saved through His Atonement.

Because Adam and Eve ate the fruit and disobeyed God, our natural selves want to sin. To change, we must follow the feelings from the Holy Ghost. Our nature changes through the Atonement of Jesus Christ. We must be like little children who are willing to listen, learn, and change.

One day soon, the whole world will know that Jesus Christ is their savior. All people will be judged for what they choose to do in this life. They will be judged for the evil or good they choose to do. Amen."

King Benjamin Invites Us To Do Good

MOSIAH 4

The people prayed to God for forgiveness of their sins after they heard King Benjamin's words. God forgave their sins because of their faith in Jesus Christ. They felt so happy.

King Benjamin continued to teach them. "Always remember how good God has been to you. Continue to repent of your sins. If you do, God will always forgive you. You will always be filled with His love.

As you learn more about what is true and right, you will always want peace. You won't let your children fight and argue with each other. You will teach them to love one another, to obey truth, to be honest, and to serve each other.

Take care of the poor and needy. Don't ever say they deserve to be poor, because aren't we all poor and needy? None of us could live without God's help. So help each other. Feed the hungry, clothe the naked, and visit the sick.

Continue to have faith and obey the commandments. Make sure your thoughts are good thoughts. Make sure your words are good words. Make sure your actions are good actions. Do these things all your life."

After King Benjamin's Sermon

MOSIAH 5-6

The people told King Benjamin the Spirit of Christ had changed their hearts. They only wanted to do good from now on. They made a covenant, or promise, to obey God's commandments.

King Benjamin said, "Your faith in Jesus Christ has changed your hearts. Because of your covenant, you will be called the children of Christ. Only Jesus Christ can save you.

You will know Jesus Christ when you do the things He asks. Be strong and faithful, and do good things, so Jesus Christ can call you His follower. If you do, you will return to live in heaven."

King Benjamin wrote down everyone's name who made a covenant with God. He also called priests to teach the people. The priests taught the people in their homes. They taught the people about the commandments of God and the promises they made to Him.

King Mosiah took over as king for his father. He was good just like King Benjamin. He also worked like King Benjamin. King Benjamin lived for three more years and then he died.

Ammon Finds the People of Zeniff

MOSIAH 7

Years before Mosiah became king, there was a man named Zeniff. He had taken a group of Nephites back to the land Lehi-Nephi. The people now wanted to know what happened to Zeniff and his people.

King Mosiah sent a man named Ammon with fifteen strong men to find the Nephites who went with Zeniff. Ammon and his men didn't know where to look. They wandered for forty days before finding Zeniff's people.

Ammon took three of his men with him to Zeniff's city. But the guards of the city tied them up and put them into prison. After two days, the king had Ammon and his men brought to him. The king's name was Limhi.

King Limhi spoke to Ammon and his men, "I am Limhi, the son of King Noah, who was the son of Zeniff. I would have killed you, but I wanted to know why you came so close to our city? Speak!"

Ammon bowed and said, "King Limhi, I thank God you did not kill us. We are from Zarahemla. We came to find Zeniff and his people." King Limhi shouted, "I am so happy! I will have my people celebrate tomorrow!

We thought that everyone in Zarahemla had died! We are enslaved by the Lamanites, but you and your men will help us escape from them." Then King Limhi sent the guards to go get the rest of Ammon's men.

King Limhi Speaks to His People

MOSIAH 7–8

The next day, King Limhi gathered his people to the temple. "My people, we pay taxes to the Lamanites, but we will soon be free! Trust in God. He will free us like He freed Moses and the Israelites from Egypt!

The Lamanite king, Laman, gave us this land. He wanted to enslave us one day. He tricked my grandfather, King Zeniff. Now we pay the Lamanites half of everything we make.

We are all suffering. Many of our people have died because we did not listen to God. God would have helped us if we had been faithful. God even sent us a prophet to warn us. But we killed His prophet instead.

God's prophet taught us about Jesus Christ. He taught us that Jesus Christ will have a body and come to earth. But because the prophet taught us that God made our bodies to look like His, we killed the prophet.

God said that He will not help His people when they
disobey. But if we trust and follow God with all our
hearts, then He will set us free."

King Limhi had Ammon speak to his people. Ammon told them what had happened in Zarahemla since Zeniff left. He even taught them what King Benjamin preached from the tower.

The Twenty-Four Jaredite Plates

MOSIAH 8

After Ammon finished speaking, Limhi sent the people home. Limhi brought Ammon the records of his people so he could read them. After Ammon read the records, Limhi told him that he had tried to find Zarahemla.

Limhi had sent a group of forty-three people to find Zarahemla. They never found Zarahemla, but found instead a land full of bones and ruined buildings. "They also found twenty-four gold plates," Limhi said.

"Can you interpret languages?" Limhi asked Ammon. "The plates have a strange language written on them." Ammon told him he could not, but that King Mosiah had the power to translate languages.

Ammon explained, "He is a seer. A seer is a prophet, someone who can see the past and the future. A seer is also someone who reveals secret and hidden things. Seers reveal things no one can know.

The only gift greater than being a seer is being given God's power. Through the faith of prophets, God can work mighty miracles among His children." Then Limhi replied, "How great are the works of God!"

Zeniff Leaves Zarahemla

MOSIAH 9

This is the record of Zeniff and his people. Zeniff was a spy for the Nephites. He needed to learn how to destroy the Lamanites. But when he saw the good things about them, he didn't want to destroy them.

Zeniff told his leader they should try to make peace with the Lamanites. Zeniff's leader was a wicked man. He tried to kill Zeniff instead. Some soldiers rescued Zeniff. The army fought each other until almost everyone was killed.

Zeniff and his soldiers returned to Zarahemla. They gathered other Nephites who wanted to return to the land of Lehi-Nephi. They traveled many days until they reached the land of Lehi-Nephi.

Laman, the Lamanite king, let Zeniff and his people build their new home in the land of Lehi-Nephi. Zeniff's people began to build buildings and a wall around the city. They planted seeds and began to grow food.

But King Laman actually wanted to enslave Zeniff's people. He let Zeniff's people build and grow food for twelve years. Then he took his army to battle and enslave Zeniff's people.

Zeniff armed his people with bows and arrows, slings, swords, clubs, and cimeters. Zeniff's people prayed to God for help. God heard their prayers and helped them defeat the Lamanites. The Lamanites left their lands.

Zeniff Fights the Lamanites

MOSIAH 10

Zeniff set guards all around the land. He wanted to protect them from another surprise attack. He had his people work hard to prepare for another attack. They made weapons, they grew food, and they made clothing.

They had peace for twenty-two years. Then King Laman died. His son became king of the Lamanites. This new king gathered the Lamanite army to go to war against Zeniff and his people again.

The Lamanites hated the Nephites. Laman and Lemuel taught their children to hate Nephi and his children. So their children taught their children. And their children taught their children.

The Lamanites believed that Nephi and his children treated Laman and Lemuel unfairly. The Lamanites were taught to fight and kill a Nephite if they could. So they now came to battle Zeniff's people.

Zeniff had all the women and children hide in the wilderness. He gathered all the men, young and old, to fight the Lamanites. Zeniff's people prayed to God. They trusted in God to protect them.

When the Lamanites arrived, Zeniff's people fought hard until they won. Countless Lamanites died in the battle. The remaining Lamanites left. Zeniff was now an old man. He made his son, Noah, king.

Wicked King Noah

MOSIAH 11

Noah was not a good man. He did not follow God's commandments. He removed his father's priests and made other wicked men his new priests.

Noah and his priests disobeyed God. They had many wives. Noah taxed his people one-fifth of everything they owned. He used the money to pay himself and the priests so they wouldn't have to work.

Noah used the tax money to build himself a palace
and throne. He built many rich buildings. He even
built tall towers to see over all the land. Noah loved
his riches. He also loved drinking wine.

Noah and his priests spent most of their time having wicked parties. Noah and his priests were bad examples. They also caused the people to become more wicked.

Soon the Lamanites began to sneak into the land. They would kill a few Nephites and take their food. Noah sent guards out, but he didn't send enough and they were all killed.

So Noah sent an army to attack the Lamanites. His army destroyed the Lamanites who had been attacking them. Noah and his people believed they had won because of their own strength, not God's.

Abinadi the Prophet
MOSIAH 11–12

In Noah's kingdom lived a man named Abinadi. God called Abinadi as a prophet to preach to the people. Abinadi preached, "Beware! I see your wickedness. If you do not repent, you will become prisoners of the Lamanites."

The people got angry and tried to kill Abinadi. God helped Abinadi escape. When King Noah heard about Abinadi, he said, "Who does he think he is? He can't judge us! Bring him to me, so I can kill him!"

After two years, Abinadi came back to preach. He said, "You will all become Lamanite prisoners! King Noah's life will be like clothes in a fire. God will let you go hungry and get sick.

You will have to carry heavy loads like pack animals. God will send hail. He will send hot, dry wind and insects to ruin your food because you are wicked. If you do not repent, you will be completely destroyed!"

The people captured Abinadi and brought him to King Noah. "King Noah, this man says that we will all be destroyed. He said you will be like clothes in a fire. We know he is a liar, so do whatever you want with him."

Abinadi Testifies against King Noah

MOSIAH 12–16

King Noah put Abinadi in prison. He gathered his priests together. They decided to question Abinadi. They wanted to trick him into saying something that wasn't true. If they could make Abinadi look guilty, then they could kill him.

King Noah brought Abinadi out of prison. The priests asked Abinadi questions about the scriptures. Abinadi replied, "Aren't you priests? Do you pretend to have the Spirit when you teach the people?

Why do you ask me what the scriptures mean? Because you don't know the truth. You haven't tried to learn it. So, what do you teach the people?" asked Abinadi. "We teach the law of Moses," said the priests.

"If you teach the law of Moses, why don't you keep it? All you care about is money. You cause your people to sin. That is why God sent me to teach you," said Abinadi.

"God will destroy you. If you keep the commandments of God, you will be saved. Have you kept the commandments? No! Have you taught your people to keep the commandments? No!"

"Take him away and kill him! This man is crazy!" Shouted King Noah. Before anyone could touch him, Abinadi said, "Do not touch me! God will kill you if you do." Abinadi glowed with light. No one dared to touch him.

"I must finish telling you what God has sent me to tell you. You are angry because I speak the truth. When I'm done, it doesn't matter what you do to me. But beware, whatever you do to me will also happen to you."

Then Abinadi told King Noah and the priests each of the ten commandments. "You have not taught the people to obey these commandments," Abinadi said. "You cannot be saved only by following the law of Moses.

The law is a symbol of Jesus Christ's Atonement, which will save us. Jesus Christ will come to live on earth to save His people. Christ will have a body. He will perform miracles.

Isaiah the prophet taught that Jesus Christ will not be handsome. Many will not listen to Him or follow Him. But because of His suffering, we can all be saved.

Abinadi continued, "Jesus Christ will be crucified and die. But He will rise from the dead. He will pay for our sins. Everyone who listens and obeys the prophets will return to live in God's kingdom.

One day, there will be a resurrection—when we will rise from the dead. The prophets, and everyone who follows them, will be the first to be resurrected. These people are the ones who have obeyed God's commandments.

Satan tricked Adam and Eve. All humankind could now sin and would someday die because Adam and Eve disobeyed God. Without Jesus Christ, no one could be saved from sin or be resurrected.

Christ is the Light and Life of the World—a light that can never be darkened. Because of Jesus Christ, we can be resurrected. Because of Jesus Christ, we can be made clean again after we have sinned.

Repent of your sins. Remember that only through Jesus Christ can you be saved. If you teach the law of Moses, then teach them that it describes what Jesus Christ will do for us. Amen."

Abinadi's Final Testimony

MOSIAH 17

When Abinadi finished speaking, King Noah commanded the priests to put him to death. There was one young priest named Alma who believed Abinadi's words. Alma asked King Noah to let Abinadi go.

King Noah got angry and sent his servants to kill Alma instead. Alma escaped and hid himself. Alma stayed hidden for many days. While hiding, Alma wrote down all the words Abinadi had said.

Abinadi went back to prison while King Noah and the priests discussed what to do. After three days, King Noah brought Abinadi out of prison. He said, "We find you guilty. If you take back what you said, we will not kill you."

"I will not take back anything I said even if it means you will kill me," said Abinadi. "Everything I said was true. If you kill me, you are killing an innocent person." Abinadi's words scared King Noah. He almost let Abinadi go.

But the priests yelled at Abinadi, "How dare you speak to the king that way!" Noah listened to the priests and sentenced Abinadi to death by fire. So Abinadi was taken and tied up.

When the fire started to burn, Abinadi prophesied to King Noah, "Someday your enemies will take you and burn you just like me. God will avenge His people. O God, receive my soul!" With that testimony, Abinadi died.

Alma at the Waters of Mormon

MOSIAH 18

Alma repented of his sins. Then he began to teach the words of Abinadi. Many people believed him. They would go to Alma's hiding place to listen to Alma teach. The place was called the Waters of Mormon.

One day, Alma was teaching the people about faith, repentance, and baptism. Alma said, "Do you wish to be called God's people? Are you willing to help each other? Are you willing to comfort those who are sad?

Are you willing to stand up for God and His teachings—no matter what? Do you want to live with God forever in heaven? If these are all things you want and are willing to do, then be baptized. And God will give you the Spirit."

The people clapped their hands and shouted, "Yes! We want all these things!" So Alma walked into the Waters of Mormon and baptized the people. They called themselves the Church of Christ.

King Noah began to notice his people leaving the city. He sent spies to follow them. When the spies told King Noah about Alma and the church, he got angry. He sent his army to destroy Alma and his followers.

God warned Alma. The members of the church gathered their families and tents and left before the army arrived. They traveled to a beautiful land with lots of clean water. They called the place Helam.

King Noah Dies

MOSIAH 19

After Alma and his people left, some of the people began to be angry with King Noah. Gideon was one of these people. He was a very strong man. He fought with King Noah. He tried to kill the king.

King Noah ran away up his tower. From the tower, King Noah saw an army of Lamanites coming. King Noah said, "Gideon, don't kill me! The Lamanites are coming. They will kill us all!" So Gideon didn't kill the king.

King Noah didn't care about his people. He only wanted to save himself. He commanded his people to run from the Lamanites. While they were running away, King Noah commanded his men to leave their families behind.

Some of the men left with King Noah and his priests. Many of the men refused to leave their families. The men who stayed asked their daughters to beg the Lamanites to not kill them. So they did.

The Lamanites listened to the Nephite daughters. Instead of killing the Nephites, they made the Nephites promise to pay them. The Nephites had to pay half of everything they owned every year. They also had to find King Noah and give him to the Lamanites.

Gideon sent a group of men to find King Noah. Gideon's men found the group who had left with King Noah, but King Noah and his priests were not with them. The men returned to the city and told Gideon what happened.

The men who went with King Noah wanted to return to protect their wives and children. Noah said they couldn't go back. This made the men angry. They took King Noah and burned him to death like Abinadi.

King Noah's priests were afraid they would be burned to death too, so they ran away. The men were on their way back to the city when they met Gideon's men trying to find King Noah.

The people decided to make King Noah's son Limhi their king. He was a good man. King Limhi promised to pay the Lamanites. The Lamanite king promised that his people wouldn't kill King Limhi's people anymore.

The Lamanite king left guards all around King Limhi's land. He didn't want King Limhi or his people to escape. So King Limhi began to have peace in the land again.

Lamanite Daughters Are Kidnapped

MOSIAH 20

There was a place called Shemlon. The Lamanite daughters would go there to sing and dance and have fun. One day, a small group went to sing and dance there. King Noah's priests were hiding close by. They watched the girls dancing and singing.

After a while, only twenty-four girls were still there. The priests kidnapped them. When the girls didn't come home, the Lamanites thought King Limhi's people had taken them. So the Lamanites went to battle King Limhi.

King Limhi had been watching the Lamanites from the tower. He saw them getting ready for war, so he prepared his people to fight. King Limhi had his army hide and wait for the Lamanites.

When the Lamanites arrived, King Limhi's army surprised them. Limhi's army was half as big as the Lamanite army. But Limhi's army fought hard to protect their families. They fought so hard, they began to win.

During the battle, they found the Lamanite king. He was wounded. The soldiers brought him to King Limhi. King Limhi asked, "Why have you attacked us and broken your promise? We have kept our promise to you."

"You kidnapped our daughters! That's why we came." King Limhi wanted to find out who in his kingdom had kidnapped the Lamanite daughters. Gideon reminded the king that Noah's priests were still hiding in the wilderness.

King Limhi told the Lamanite king about the priests. "Take me to my army, so I can tell them to stop fighting your people." The Lamanite King told his army to stop fighting. They returned to their own land.

King Limhi's People Suffer

MOSIAH 21

The Lamanite king left soldiers to guard Limhi's people. The soldiers were angry with Limhi and his people. They made Limhi's people work hard. They would even slap them on the face.

Limhi's people became frustrated. They decided to fight back. They gathered their army to fight the Lamanites. They battled the Lamanites three times. They lost each time. Many of the men died.

Limhi's people began to pray to God for help. God helped them, but He did not free them because of their sins. God blessed their fields and flocks to make more food, so they wouldn't go hungry.

Limhi commanded his people to give to the poor and needy. So many men had died that there were many widows and fatherless children who needed help and food.

The priests of King Noah began to sneak into the city and steal food. So King Limhi began to lock the food up. King Limhi set guards around to keep watch. They wanted to catch the priests and punish them.

One day, King Limhi was outside the city walls with his guards. A group of men came toward the city. King Limhi thought they were the priests of King Noah, so he captured them.

The men were not the priests. They were Ammon
and his men from Zarahemla. They were searching
for Zeniff and his people. King Limhi told Ammon
everything that had happened to them since Zeniff
had left Zarahemla.

King Limhi told Ammon about Abinadi. King Limhi and his people repented and wanted to be baptized. They made a promise to follow God's commandments. But with Abinadi and Alma gone, there was no one who had authority to baptize.

King Limhi's People Escape

MOSIAH 22

Ammon and King Limhi tried to find a way to free the people from the Lamanites. Fighting hadn't worked. The only way was for everyone to escape and go to Zarahemla.

There were Lamanite guards surrounding the city. King Limhi gathered the people together. He asked them for ideas on how to escape. Gideon had an idea. They would get the Lamanites drunk and escape.

So King Limhi sent Gideon to the Lamanite camp with lots of wine as a gift. While the Lamanites got drunk, the people gathered all their things and waited. When the Lamanites fell asleep, the people escaped out of the back city gates.

When the Lamanites woke up, they chased after them. After two days, the Lamanites got lost. King Limhi and his people traveled for many days until they reached Zarahemla. King Mosiah was glad to have them join his people.

Alma and His People Build Helam

MOSIAH 23

Alma and his followers had escaped King Noah's army. They traveled for eight days. They found a beautiful land with lots of clean water. They called the place Helam. They pitched their tents and began to build a city.

The people wanted Alma to be their king. Alma refused, "We just escaped wicked King Noah. We don't want to have kings. We should only follow and listen to teachers who follow the commandments and God."

Alma taught them to keep the commandments of God. He taught them to love each other. They soon began to be rich and have many things. Their priests and teachers taught them to be good.

God decided to test Alma and his people. God gives His people trials to test their patience and their faith. So one day, an army of Lamanites arrived at the city. Alma told the people not to be afraid and to remember God.

The people prayed, asking God to make the Lamanites not want to kill them. God listened. The Lamanites were lost and wanted to know how to return home. They promised to leave if Alma showed them the way.

This Lamanite army was the same one chasing King Limhi and his people. After they got lost, they found King Noah's priests and the kidnapped Lamanite daughters. The leader of the priests was named Amulon.

Amulon and the priests were now married to the Lamanite daughters. They joined the Lamanite army. The Lamanites were trying to find their way home when they came across Alma's city of Helam.

Alma showed the Lamanites how to return home. The Lamanites did not keep their promise. Laman, the Lamanite king, put guards around the land of Helam. He also left Amulon in charge of the city.

Alma and His People Escape from Amulon

MOSIAH 24

Amulon was a wicked man. He used to be one of King Noah's priests, just like Alma. He did not like Alma. Amulon forced Alma and his people to work. The tasks they had to do were very difficult.

The people began to pray for help. Amulon did not want them to pray. He commanded his guards to kill anyone who prayed. So Alma and the people began to pray silently in their hearts. God comforted them.

God promised to help Alma and the people. God made the difficult tasks feel easy to them. The people continued to work with faith, patience, and happiness. Soon, God promised to help them escape.

One night, God told Alma and his people to gather their things. In the early morning, God made all the guards fall asleep. So Alma and his people escaped. They traveled all day until they reached a valley called Alma.

The people prayed and gave thanks to God. God warned them to keep going because the guards had woken up. So Alma and his people traveled for twelve more days. They finally reached Zarahemla and joined King Mosiah and the other Nephites.

Mulek and Zarahemla

MOSIAH 25

In Zarahemla, there were two groups of people: the Nephites and the Mulekites. King Mosiah gathered them all together. Mosiah and others read to the people the records of Zeniff and Limhi's people and Alma and his converts.

The people were amazed. The people thanked God for His goodness. They felt sad for the wickedness of the Lamanites. But they also felt joy because Alma and his people had escaped.

King Mosiah asked Alma to preach to the people. So Alma taught the people about faith and repentance. Many of the people wanted to be baptized, including King Limhi and his people. So Alma baptized them.

Then King Mosiah had Alma set up churches throughout the land. Alma set up seven churches. They were all part of the same religion. They were called the people of God, and God blessed them.

Alma Becomes High Priest

MOSIAH 26

King Mosiah made Alma the leader of the Church. He was called the high priest. Many teenagers and young adults in the church did not believe in Jesus Christ. They chose to leave the church.

These people spoke to many members. The things they said caused some members to be confused and to sin. Several teachers and priests in the church brought these members to Alma.

Alma didn't know what to do. He brought them to King Mosiah. Mosiah said that Alma needed to judge them. Alma didn't want to judge them wrongly, so he prayed for help. God spoke to Alma, "You are blessed, Alma.

You had faith in Abinadi's words. You established My church. I promise you eternal life. You will gather My people into the church. Baptize anyone who repents of their sins. They will become members of My church.

For members who sin, if they tell you their sins and truly repent, forgive them. As many times as they repent, forgive them. When someone does wrong against you, forgive them.

If someone does not repent, they cannot be a member of My church." Alma wrote down God's words to remember them. He judged the members who had sinned. If they repented, he forgave them.

Alma the Younger and the Sons of Mosiah

MOSIAH 27

Many unbelievers pestered the members of the church. Some of these unbelievers were King Mosiah's sons: Ammon, Aaron, Omner, and Himni. One of Alma's sons, Alma the Younger, was also one these unbelievers.

Alma the Younger was very good at speaking. He used his words to cause many people to leave the church and sin. Alma and the sons of Mosiah secretly tried to make members leave to destroy the Church of Jesus Christ.

One day, while they were trying to destroy the church, an angel of God appeared to them. The angel's voice shook the earth. Alma and the sons of Mosiah fell to the ground with surprise. The angel said, "Alma, stand!

Why do you try to destroy the church? God will not
let His church be destroyed. Your father and the
members have prayed to God. They pray you will
learn the truth. I have come to answer their prayers.

Do not try to destroy the church anymore." Then the angel left. Alma was so shocked that he fell down. He couldn't speak or move. The sons of Mosiah picked him up and brought him back to his father.

His father, Alma, was so happy. His prayer was answered. He asked others to fast and pray for Alma the Younger. After two days, Alma the Younger began to speak. "I have repented of my sins. I have been born again!

Jesus Christ told me we must change our natural selves. We must be spiritually reborn—become righteous. If we aren't reborn, if we don't become righteous, we cannot return to live with God."

Alma the Younger and the sons of Mosiah began to teach the people about their experience with the angel. They taught the people to obey God's commandments. Many listened and gained a testimony of Jesus Christ.

The Sons of Mosiah Become Missionaries

MOSIAH 28

The sons of Mosiah wanted to teach the Lamanites. They asked their father, King Mosiah, if they could go. They believed the Lamanites and Nephites would become friends if they knew about Jesus Christ.

They wanted to help every human be saved through Jesus Christ. The sons of Mosiah begged their father for many days to let them go. King Mosiah prayed to ask God what he should do.

God spoke to Mosiah, "Let them go. Many will believe their teachings. I will protect them." So King Mosiah gave his sons permission to go. The sons of Mosiah packed and began to travel to the Lamanite lands.

King Mosiah Translates
the Jaredite Plates

MOSIAH 28

The people of Zarahemla wanted to know what was written on the gold plates King Limhi's people had found. So King Mosiah began to translate the plates using two special stones.

The plates told the story of a group of people who left from the Tower of Babel. They were called Jaredites. They traveled to this land where they destroyed themselves. King Mosiah shared the records with the people of Zarahemla.

King Mosiah took the Jaredite records and all the records of Nephi and gave them to Alma the Younger. He told Alma the Younger to keep them safe. He also told him to start keeping a record of their people.

Alma the Younger Becomes Chief Judge

MOSIAH 29

The people wanted Aaron, King Mosiah's son, to be king after King Mosiah. Aaron, nor any of King Mosiah's sons, wanted to be king. So King Mosiah wrote a letter to his people about what they should do.

"My people, I will be your king until I die. After I am gone, let us no longer have a king. Good kings are good. But remember wicked King Noah? He caused his people to sin. His people became enslaved by the Lamanites.

Instead of kings, we will have judges. The people will vote who their judges will be. Because most people are good, the people will choose good judges. Then, the judges will use our laws to judge.

If a judge isn't good, we will have a higher judge
judge the lower judge. If a higher judge isn't good,
a group of lower judges will judge the higher judge.
I want this to be a free land where everyone can
enjoy the same rights and freedoms."

The people agreed with King Mosiah. They were excited that everyone would be equal. They loved King Mosiah for giving them this freedom. They gathered together and began to vote for their judges.

The people voted for Alma the Younger to be the chief judge over all the people. Alma was also the high priest over the church. He was a good man who followed God's commandments.

The reign of the judges began with Alma the Younger as chief judge. Soon, King Mosiah and Alma the Elder died. With King Mosiah's death, the reign of the Nephite kings ended.

NOTE TO PARENTS

PURPOSE

The goal of this book is to engage young children in the stories of the Book of Mormon. It is not meant to replace your reading and study of the actual text of the Book of Mormon. It is my hope that as you use this book in Family Home Evening lessons, as a resource in your family scripture studies, or just as a bedtime storybook, that it will spark gospel discussions between you and your child. Ultimately, I hope that this book will help you and your child strengthen your testimonies of Christ as the Savior and Redeemer of all humankind.

CONSTRAINTS

Adapting the Book of Mormon text into simpler language means that many of the details and nuances from the stories had to be left out. Additionally, retelling the stories was my primary intent, not interpreting the doctrines contained in the Book of Mormon. However, it is impossible, nor the intent of this book, to completely decouple the stories from the doctrines they illustrate. So, where I do address doctrines, I try to focus on the most foundational doctrines, such as the gospel of Jesus Christ, and I try to strictly adhere to the interpretations of the scriptures as written in Church-published materials. (See the end of this note for a complete list of publications referenced during this project.)

INTERPRETIVE CHOICES

There are two sections in this first volume where I decided to deviate from the normal pattern of the narrative.

The first departure is my interpretation of 2 Nephi 9 entitled in this volume as "Jacob and the Gospel." For this story, I chose to address key gospel principles that are not actually addressed in 2 Nephi 9 of the Book of Mormon. To be clear, all of the doctrines I do address are taught throughout the Book of Mormon, but in order to make the gospel principles taught in a cohesive way, I decided to consolidate them here in this one story. The ultimate goal is that the principles of the gospel of Jesus Christ will be more understandable when all shared in relation to each other.

The second departure occurs in the Isaiah chapters in 2 Nephi. Due to Isaiah's prolific use of repetition (specifically chiasmic patterns), extensive motifs, and metaphors, I had to make several organizational and interpretive choices that hopefully will help clarify some of Isaiah's warnings and prophecies for the latter-days. The referenced chapters are not necessarily sequential in this section. Additionally, many of Isaiah's teachings are not included; however, I did try to address the major themes and key teachings of those chapters. These included Isaiah's call as a prophet, the scattering and gathering of Israel, and his prophecies of the last days.

All of my interpretations of Isaiah's words were primarily taken from the Church's institute manual on the Book of Mormon and general conference talks given by current and former apostles and prophets (accessed through scriptures.byu.edu).

Additionally, portions of these stories are not included in the scriptures at all, but are rather descriptions of the historical context in which Isaiah lived, to better help explain the context of Isaiah's words. For these sections, I primarily referenced a book entitled *Isaiah: Prophet, Seer, and Poet* written by Brigham Young University's foremost scholar on Isaiah, Victor Ludlow.

ENDING THOUGHTS

Finally, I would like to say that this whole project began as a way for me to help my own children understand the stories and gospel principles of the Book of Mormon. It has been inspiring as I have written and rewritten these stories to hear my own children understanding key gospel topics and likening the scripture stories to themselves and their everyday lives. It is my hope that reading this book will spark similar gospel discussions in your own home and, ultimately, strengthen your children's testimonies.

REFERENCES

1. *The Book of Mormon: Another Testament of Jesus Christ.* Salt Lake City: The Church of Jesus Christ of Latter-day Saints, 1981.

2. *Book of Mormon Student Manual: Religion 121–122.* Salt Lake City: The Church of Jesus Christ of Latter-day Saints, 2009.

3. *Gospel Principles.* Salt Lake City: The Church of Jesus Christ of Latter-day Saints, 2009.

4. James Strong. *The New Strong's Expanded Exhaustive Concordance of the Bible.* Nashville: Thomas Nelson, 2001.

5. *Preach My Gospel.* Salt Lake City: The Church of Jesus Christ of Latter-day Saints, 2004.

6. *True to the Faith.* Salt Lake City: The Church of Jesus Christ of Latter-day Saints, 2004.

7. Victor L. Ludlow. *Isaiah: Prophet, Seer, and Poet.* Salt Lake City: Deseret Book, 1982.

About the Author and Illustrator

AUTHOR

Jason Zippro holds a master's degree in education from the University of Missouri-Saint Louis, a master's degree in business administration from the University of Utah, and a bachelor of arts degree in Italian with a minor in English and editing from Brigham Young University. Jason worked as an editor for four years before teaching 8th grade English for three years in Kansas City with the non-profit Teach for America. Jason and his wife, Sharolee, have four young children.

ILLUSTRATOR

Alycia Pace graduated from Brigham Young University with a bachelor of fine arts degree in animation and is a freelance illustrator from her home in Utah. She has written and illustrated several books including *Polly the Perfectly Polite Pig* and *How to Train a Dinosaur to Use the Potty*. She loves the smell of bookstores and exploring new places with her two children and adventurous husband.

BOOK OF MORMON
STORIES *for* KIDS

VOLUME TWO • ALMA

This book belongs to:

_____

BOOK OF MORMON

STORIES *for* KIDS

VOLUME TWO • ALMA

Text adapted by Jason Zippro

Illustrated by Alycia Pace

ISBN 13: 978-1-7349053-3-5

REL046000 RELIGION / Christianity / Church of Jesus Christ of Latter-day Saints (Mormon)
REL091000 RELIGION / Christian Education / Children & Youth
JNF049200 JUVENILE NONFICTION / Religious / Christian / Early Readers

Cover design © 2021 Primary Scriptures, LLC
Illustrations by Alycia Pace
Cover design by Angela Baxter
Edited and typeset by Emily Chambers and Kaitlin Barwick

Distributed by

CEDAR FORT
Publishing & Media

10 9 8 7 6 5 4 3 2 1

www.PrimaryScriptures.com

CONTENTS

CONTENTS

CONTENTS

ALMA

Nehor and Priestcraft
ALMA 1

In the first year of the judges, there was a large and strong Nephite named Nehor. He taught that priests should get paid for teaching. He taught that priests should be famous.

He also taught that God would save everyone. Many people believed Nehor. They began to pay him to teach. He formed his own church. He began to wear very nice clothes.

One day Nehor tried to get some members to leave the church. He found a teacher in the church and began to argue with him. The teacher was Gideon, the man who had helped Limhi and his people escape from the Lamanites.

Nehor argued with Gideon. But Gideon preached the truth to Nehor. Nehor became frustrated. He took out his sword and started to attack Gideon. Gideon was too old to protect himself and was killed.

The people took Nehor to Alma, the chief judge. Alma told Nehor, "You have pretended to preach the word of God so you could become rich and famous. This is called priestcraft.

You also tried to enforce your priestcraft by killing a righteous man. If we all try to force our beliefs on each other, then it would destroy the Nephites. You killed Gideon. The law that King Mosiah left us says that you must die."

Before he died, Nehor confessed that what he had
taught was not true. Many Nephites wanted to be
rich and famous like Nehor. These Nephites also
began to teach things that were not true.

They became false priests. Many people followed them. The false priests bullied members of the church. Some members began to get frustrated. They started to argue with the false priests. Some even got into fights.

Many members left the church because of the false priests. But many members stayed and obeyed the commandments. These members were patient even when others bullied them.

The members met together to teach and learn from each other. Because of their obedience, God blessed them with more than they needed. The members helped the poor, the sick, and the needy even if they were not members.

Amlici's Rebellion

ALMA 2–3

O ne of Nehor's followers was a man named Amlici. He was a very smart man. In year five of the judges, Amlici began to be very powerful. He had many followers who believed in the things that he taught.

Amlici's followers wanted him to be their king. The members of the church did not. They knew that Amlici wanted to destroy the church. If he became king, he would take away their churches.

The Nephites gathered together and discussed Amlici becoming their king. Finally, the people voted to see if Amlici would be king. The judges counted their votes. Amlici lost and did not become king.

This made everyone who voted against Amlici very happy. But Amlici and his followers were angry. Amlici's followers decided to make Amlici their king anyway. They called themselves Amlicites.

Amlici gathered his people together and commanded his people to attack the Nephites. Alma, the chief judge, gathered his people to defend themselves. The Nephites and Amlicites battled on a hill next to Zarahemla.

When the Amlicites began to lose, they ran away. Alma sent men to follow and spy on Amlici and his followers. In the morning, the spies returned with terrible news. The Amlicites joined an army of Lamanites.

The Nephites hurried back to Zarahemla. Next to Zarahemla was a river named Sidon. Before the Nephites finished crossing the river to Zarahemla, the Lamanite army arrived. They began to battle along the river's edge.

Alma fought with Amlici. Alma prayed to God for protection. He wanted to live to preach the gospel to the Nephites. God gave Alma strength. Alma defeated Amlici. Then Alma began to battle with the Lamanite king.

The Nephites began to win the battle. The Lamanite army ran away. So many Lamanites, Amlicites, and Nephites died that they couldn't even count them all. Many women, children, and animals had also died in the battle.

Alma Begins to Preach

ALMA 4

There were no battles in year six of the judges. But the Nephites suffered because they had lost so many people. They had also lost a lot of their animals and food.

The Nephites believed God had punished them for not being more righteous. So members of the church began to work hard to build up the church. Many Nephites chose to be baptized. They were baptized in the river Sidon.

In year eight of the judges, the people began to be rich and prideful again. Even members of the church stopped caring for the poor and the needy. Many people didn't join the church because of how the members were acting.

Alma was very worried. He decided to not be chief judge anymore. He picked a righteous elder of the church to be chief judge. His name was Nephihah. The people voted and Nephihah became the chief judge.

In year nine of the judges, Nephihah took over as chief judge. Alma stayed high priest over the church. Alma began to preach to the Nephites. He wanted to help them repent and keep God's commandments.

Alma Preaches in Zarahemla

ALMA 5

Alma chose to spend all his time teaching the Nephites the word of God. He started in Zarahemla. "I am Alma. My father made me high priest over the church. My father formed the church in the land of Nephi.

My father baptized in the Waters of Mormon. He and the members of the church escaped King Noah and the Lamanites. They came and built the church here in Zarahemla.

My father, Alma, and his people were once wicked. Being wicked is like having your spirit locked in chains. Were their spirits freed from these spiritual chains? Yes! How were they freed from their spiritual chains?

Well, my father, Alma, heard and believed in the prophet Abinadi's words. My father had a mighty change of heart. He taught the people Abinadi's words, and they also had a mighty change of heart.

They changed from wanting to be wicked to wanting to do good. This is the mighty change in their hearts. As soon as they wanted to be good, their spirits were freed from their spiritual chains.

This is what happened to my father, Alma, and your parents. What about you? Have you had a mighty change of heart? If so, do you still feel that desire to always do good and not be wicked?

Do you have faith in Jesus Christ? Have you stopped thinking you're better than others? Have you stopped wishing you had what others have? Have you stopped making fun of others and talking behind their backs?

Do you see Jesus Christ's reflection in yourself? If not, you must prepare and repent quickly. Soon there will be no more time to repent. So repent! Repent so that you can be saved and live with God in heaven.

We are like sheep. If we do good things and listen to Jesus Christ, we are part of His flock. If we are wicked, we are lost sheep without a shepherd. Everything good comes from God, and everything evil comes from Satan.

I know that Jesus Christ will come and take away our sins. If you believe and follow Him until the end, He will forgive you of your sins. The Spirit told me to tell you to repent!

Will you stop ignoring God? Will you stop worrying about being rich? Will you stop worrying about what others think of you? If you will listen to Jesus Christ, He will make you one of His sheep. Repent and be baptized."

Alma Preaches in Gideon

ALMA 6–7

After Alma finished preaching to the church in Zarahemla, he left to visit other cities. The first city he went to was Gideon. Alma began to preach to the people in Gideon.

"My dear members of the church in Gideon, I hope that you worship God and not idols. There are many things to come, but the most important thing is that Jesus Christ will soon come to live on earth.

The Spirit didn't tell me He would come to live with us. But the Spirit did say repent! Get ready for His coming. He will be born in Jerusalem to a woman named Mary. She will give birth to the Son of God.

Jesus Christ will be tempted and suffer much pain in His life. He will take on death for us. He will suffer for our sins, so that He can forgive us of our sins. This is my testimony.

So repent and be baptized, so your sins can be washed away. Have faith in Jesus Christ. He can make you clean from all your sins. Promise to keep God's commandments by being baptized. Then you will have eternal life.

Have faith, hope, and charity. Continue to do good things. Now, God will bless you with peace over your families, your houses, your lands, and your animals forever. Amen."

Alma Preaches in Ammonihah

ALMA 8

Alma went home to Zarahemla after teaching in Gideon. At the beginning of year ten of the judges, Alma taught in a city called Melek. Many people in Melek listened and were baptized. Then Alma went to the city Ammonihah.

Alma began to preach in Ammonihah. But the people there were wicked and did not want to listen to a prophet. They threw Alma out of their city. Alma fasted and prayed for them. He went to go preach somewhere else.

While Alma was traveling, an angel appeared to him. The angel said, "You are blessed, Alma. You have kept God's commandments ever since I appeared to you the first time. Now go back and preach to the people of Ammonihah."

Alma quickly returned to Ammonihah. Alma was hungry. He asked a man for some food. The man said, "I know you are a prophet of God. An angel told me you would come. Come to my home, and I will feed you."

The man's name was Amulek. Alma stayed with Amulek for several days. Then God told Alma to take Amulek with him to preach again to the people of Ammonihah. They were both filled with the Holy Ghost.

Alma, Amulek, and Zeezrom

ALMA 9–13

Alma began to preach to the people. The people said, "Why would God send only one person to teach us?" Alma replied, "You are all wicked. If you don't repent, God will completely destroy you all.

Don't you remember what God told Lehi? 'If you keep My commandments, you will do well in this land.' If you don't keep the commandments and repent, the Lamanites will come and destroy you."

The people got angry with Alma for calling them wicked. They wanted to put Alma in prison, but Amulek began to speak to them. "I am Amulek. Many of you know me. Because of my hard work, I have become rich.

But I have also been wicked. I have not paid attention to the things of God. The other day, an angel appeared to me. He said I would meet a prophet asking for food. He said I should take him home.

On my way home, I ran into this man who is speaking to you. His name is Alma. I know he is a prophet of God because an angel told me so. What he is saying is true. He has blessed my family while staying in my home."

When Amulek finished speaking, many people were amazed. They were surprised that more than one witness was saying they were wicked. There were some lawyers in the crowd who didn't like what Amulek said.

One of these lawyers was Zeezrom. Zeezrom wanted to send Alma and Amulek to prison. Zeezrom decided he would trick them. He told Amulek, "Here is a bag full of silver coins. I will give it to you if you say God doesn't exist."

Amulek replied, "Don't you know that someone righteous would never do that? You know there is a God, but you love money more than Him." Zeezrom asked, "So if there is a God, will He save the people in their sins?"

"God cannot save the wicked. Let me teach you. There are two different deaths. When our bodies die, that is one kind of death. But our bodies and spirits will be reunited thanks to Jesus Christ. This is called resurrection.

Everyone will be resurrected, even the wicked," explained Amulek. Alma continued, "What Amulek has taught is true. But if we are wicked, then we will also have a second death. A spiritual death.

After we die, God will judge us. If we were wicked, we will be cast out with Satan. If we do not repent and obey the commandments, then Jesus Christ cannot save us. Repent, so you will not have to suffer a spiritual death."

Zeezrom was silent. He began to feel guilty for trying to trick Alma and Amulek. Alma said, "God has told me your thoughts. I know you tried to trick us with your words." Zeezrom was amazed and began to shake with fear.

One of the chief rulers of Ammonihah was in the crowd. His name was Antionah. He asked, "Can you explain more? You say we will be resurrected, but God stopped Adam and Eve from living forever."

Alma explained, "After Adam and Eve ate the fruit from the tree of knowledge of good and evil, God didn't let them eat from the tree of life. If they had eaten from both, then they would have lived.

God gave us this life so we can prepare to live forever with Him. He sent angels to teach us of His plan. His plan is to have us repent of our sins. If we repent, He will forgive us of our sins.

God called priests to teach us His plan. Before this life on earth, these priests were faithful and obedient. They learned to be priests in this life. The greatest of all these priests was Melchizedek. Now repent!"

Alma and Amulek in Prison

ALMA 14

Alma and Amulek finished speaking to the people of Ammonihah. Many believed their words. But there were many others who called Alma and Amulek liars. They wanted to destroy Alma and Amulek.

They were angry because Alma and Amulek had preached against their wickedness. So the people brought them to the chief judge of Ammonihah. They spoke against Alma and Amulek.

Zeezrom began to feel very guilty. He heard the people using his words to testify against Alma and Amulek. He tried to fix his mistake by saying, "No! I am guilty. These men are innocent." He tried to save Alma and Amulek.

The people cast Zeezrom and some of the believers out of the city. They sent men to throw stones at them. They threw some of the believers into a pit of fire. They threw their scriptures into the fire with them.

The chief judge of Ammonihah and many of the lawyers, judges, and priests followed Nehor's teachings. These wicked men tied Alma and Amulek up and put them in prison.

After three days, many of these wicked men came to the prison. They slapped Alma and Amulek on the face. They spit on them. They took away their food, water, and clothes so they would be hungry, thirsty, and naked.

Many days later, the chief judge and wicked men came again. The chief judge said, "If you really have the power of God, free yourselves from these bands. If you can, then we will believe that God will destroy us as you preached."

Alma stood and prayed out loud, "O God, give us strength through our faith in Jesus Christ to be freed." Then Alma and Amulek immediately broke their bands. When the chief judge and wicked men saw this, they became very afraid.

The prison began to shake and fall apart. The chief judge and wicked men tried to escape. The prison fell on top of them and killed them. Only Alma and Amulek were not killed because God protected them.

The rest of the people of Ammonihah came to see what had happened. When they saw that only Alma and Amulek were alive, they ran away in fear. God commanded Alma and Amulek to leave the city. So Alma and Amulek obeyed.

Zeezrom Joins the Church

ALMA 15

After Alma and Amulek left Ammonihah, they came to a land called Sidom. The people who had been kicked out of Ammonihah were in Sidom. Zeezrom was also there.

Zeezrom thought that Alma and Amulek had died because of what he had done. He felt so bad that he got sick with a fever. When he heard they were not dead, he sent a message to have them come to him.

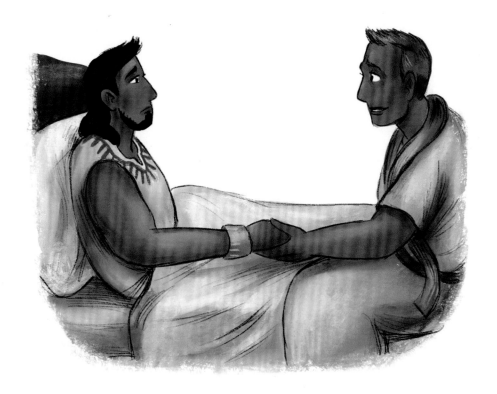

When they came, Zeezrom reached out to them. He asked them to heal him. Alma took his hand and said, "Do you believe Jesus Christ has the power to save?" Zeezrom said, "I believe everything you have taught."

Alma prayed, "God, please forgive this man. If he has enough faith in Jesus Christ, please heal him." Zeezrom jumped out of bed. Everyone was surprised. They went and told everyone what happened.

Alma baptized Zeezrom. Zeezrom began to preach the gospel to the people in Sidom. Alma set up a church in Sidom. People from all over the land came and were baptized.

But the people in Ammonihah did not come to be baptized. Amulek had to give up all his things and leave them in Ammonihah. All of Amulek's friends and family rejected Amulek, even his own father.

When Alma and Amulek finished setting up the church in Sidom, Alma took Amulek back to Zarahemla. Amulek stayed in Alma's home. Alma comforted Amulek because of everything he had lost.

Lamanites Destroy Ammonihah

ALMA 16

In year eleven of the judges, the Lamanites attacked the Nephites. They started at the city of Ammonihah. The Lamanite army destroyed Ammonihah before the Nephites could gather their army.

The Lamanite army destroyed the entire city of Ammonihah in one day. No one from the city survived. None of the Nephites wanted to live there anymore. They called it the land of Desolation of Nehors.

The Lamanite army also took many Nephites as
prisoners from the land of Noah. The chief captain
of the Nephite army was named Zoram. He wanted
to get the Nephite prisoners back.

Zoram knew that Alma was a prophet. Zoram asked Alma where he should go to free the captive Nephites. Alma prayed to God. God told Alma where to send the Nephite army.

Alma told Zoram where to go. Zoram and the Nephite army left and found the Lamanite army where God said they would be. The Lamanite army ran away. Every Nephite prisoner was freed.

The Church Grows Strong

ALMA 16

In years twelve, thirteen, and fourteen of the judges, the Nephites had peace. Alma and Amulek began to travel. They taught the people in their temples and churches. They called many others to help them teach.

Alma, Amulek, and other priests taught to not lie or trick others. They taught the people to be happy with what they have, even if their neighbor has something they want. They taught them not to steal or kill.

The people became righteous. They asked where Jesus Christ would come to earth. They were taught that Jesus Christ would appear to them after He was resurrected. This made the people joyful.

Alma Reunites with the Sons of Mosiah

ALMA 17

In year fourteen of the judges, Alma traveled from Gideon to Manti. While Alma was traveling, he came across the sons of Mosiah. They hadn't seen each other in fourteen years.

The sons of Mosiah had been missionaries. They had been in the land of the Lamanites. They had prayed, fasted, and searched the scriptures. Alma was happy to see they were still righteous.

The Sons of Mosiah Split Up

ALMA 17

In year one of the judges, the sons of Mosiah asked king Mosiah if they could go teach the Lamanites. God told King Mosiah that they would be safe. So the sons of Mosiah traveled to the Lamanite lands.

The sons of Mosiah wanted everyone to know about God, even the Lamanites. Other missionaries went with the sons of Mosiah. As they traveled, they fasted and prayed for the Spirit. God comforted them.

God spoke to them, "Go. Teach the Lamanites. Be patient in your struggles. They will know me through your examples. If you are patient and trust in me, many Lamanites will become members."

Soon the group arrived at the borders of the Lamanite lands. Ammon spoke to them and blessed them. They trusted God would help them meet again after their missions. Then they all went in different directions.

Ammon Protects
King Lamoni's Flocks

ALMA 17

Ammon went to the land of Ishmael. The Lamanites there brought him to their king, Lamoni. Ammon told the king that he wanted to be his servant. So King Lamoni had Ammon help watch over his flocks.

One day, Ammon and the other Lamanite servants brought the flocks to drink water. There was a group of Lamanite men there. The men scattered all the flocks away. The Lamanite servants began to cry.

When Ammon saw them crying, he thought, "I will show God's power to these servants by saving the flocks. Then they will believe my words when I teach them about God." So Ammon spoke to the servants.

"Brothers, be glad. Let us find the flocks and gather them back together. That way, King Lamoni won't kill us for losing them." The servants agreed. They quickly ran after the flocks. Soon, they had gathered the entire flock again.

The Lamanite men were waiting by the water when Ammon and the servants returned. So Ammon slung stones at them. He killed six of them. This amazed and angered the Lamanite men. They picked up their clubs to kill Ammon.

Every time one of the Lamanite men tried to kill Ammon, Ammon cut off his arm. After many of their arms had been cut off, the Lamanite men ran away. Then Ammon and the servants watered the king's flocks.

Ammon Teaches King Lamoni

ALMA 18

The servants gathered the arms and brought them to King Lamoni. King Lamoni was surprised by Ammon's power. King Lamoni said, "He can't just be a man. He must be the Great Spirit!"

While the servants were talking with the king, Ammon had been taking care of the king's animals. Ammon finished and came to the king. Ammon asked what he should work on next.

"Who are you? Are you the Great Spirit?" asked King Lamoni. "I am not," said Ammon. "How did you defend my flocks? If you tell me, I will give you whatever you ask," Lamoni said. Ammon replied, "If I tell you, will you do as I ask?"

"Yes," said the king. Ammon explained, "The Great Spirit is God. He has called me to teach your people about Him. His Spirit gives me knowledge and power based on my faith."

Then Ammon taught King Lamoni about the Creation, the Fall of Adam and Eve, and the Atonement of Jesus Christ. After King Lamoni had heard all these things, he believed Ammon's words.

King Lamoni said, "God, be kind to my people and forgive them like You have done with the Nephites!" When he said this, he fell to the ground. He looked like he was dead. The servants brought him to the queen.

The servants laid King Lamoni's body on a bed. His body lay there for two days and two nights. The queen and her children cried and were sad because they thought King Lamoni might be dead.

King Lamoni's Household Is Converted

ALMA 19

After two days, they were going to put King Lamoni's body in a tomb. The servants of the queen told her about Ammon and his power. So the queen called Ammon to speak with her.

"My servants told me you are a prophet. They told me you have the power to do great things. Some people say my husband is dead and should be buried. I don't think he's dead. Will you look at him?"

Ammon knew that King Lamoni wasn't dead. He knew that God was working a miracle. So Ammon looked at the king and said, "The king is not dead. God put him to sleep. Don't bury him. He will wake up tomorrow."

The queen sat by the king all night. The next day, the king awoke. Ammon and the servants who saved the flocks were there. The king sat up and said to the queen, "Bless God's name! You are blessed, my queen!

I have seen Jesus Christ. He will be born and save everyone who will believe Him." The king was so full of the Spirit that he fell back down. The queen also was filled with the Spirit, and she fell down.

Ammon saw that the king and queen were filled with the Spirit. He began to pray. He was filled with the Spirit and fell to the ground too. The servants all began to pray. Soon all the servants fell to the ground from the Spirit.

The only person who hadn't fallen down was a Lamanite woman named Abish. Her father had seen a vision. Because of this vision, Abish already believed in Jesus Christ. She had kept her belief secret though.

Abish saw the servants, queen, king, and Ammon lying as if they were asleep. She quickly left and ran from house to house telling the people what happened. She wanted them to come see so they would believe in the power of God.

The people gathered together and saw the king, queen, and servants lying on the ground. They began to argue. Some thought the king and queen were punished by God for letting Ammon stay.

One man was angry with Ammon. Ammon had killed his brother while protecting the king's flocks. The man walked over to Ammon. He took out his sword. He lifted up his sword to kill Ammon, but God protected Ammon.

The man fell down dead instead. When the people saw this, they were afraid to touch anyone. They argued with each other. Some thought Ammon was a monster. Others thought he was the Great Spirit.

While the people were arguing with each other, Abish returned. She heard them arguing and began to cry. She went over to the queen and touched her hand. The queen awoke, stood up, and shouted, "Bless Jesus Christ!"

The queen reached over and touched the king's hand. He awoke and stood up. He immediately began to teach his people what Ammon taught him. Many believed the king, but many did not.

When Ammon awoke, he taught them too. Everyone who believed was baptized. They began to teach each other. They organized a church. The people of King Lamoni became a righteous people.

King Lamoni's Father

ALMA 20

One day, King Lamoni asked Ammon to go with him. He wanted Ammon to meet his father, the king of all the Lamanites. But God told Ammon not to go. Instead, God wanted Ammon to go to Middoni.

God told Ammon that his brother Aaron and his companions were in prison in Middoni. Ammon told King Lamoni. "I will go with you," said King Lamoni. "I am friends with the king of Middoni."

On their way to Middoni, Ammon and Lamoni met Lamoni's father. The king of all the Lamanites was coming to visit his son. "Where are you going with this lying Nephite?" the king asked Lamoni.

"We're going to Middoni to free his brother from prison." "No," said the king. "You will kill this Nephite and come back with me to your kingdom." Lamoni replied, "No, I will not kill him. And I will go to Middoni."

This made the king angry. He took out his sword to fight his son. Ammon stepped between them and said, "If you kill your son, you will kill an innocent man!" "Then I'll kill you instead!" shouted the king.

The king and Ammon fought with their swords. Ammon cut the king's arm so he couldn't hold his sword anymore. The king begged Ammon to not kill him. "I will give you half of my kingdom if you let me live!"

Ammon said, "All I want from you is to set my brother free from prison. And I don't want you to be angry with your son, Lamoni. Let him live his life the way he chooses." The king was shocked that Ammon didn't ask for more.

"Your brother may go free, and Lamoni will be ruler over his kingdom." The king was amazed by how much Ammon loved Lamoni. "I want you and your brothers to come visit me. I want to learn more."

Ammon and Lamoni continued to Middoni. Lamoni convinced the king of Middoni to let Aaron and his companions free. Ammon was sad to see how much his brother and companions had suffered. But they had been patient like God had told them to be.

Aaron and the Amalekites

ALMA 21

After the sons of Mosiah split up, Aaron went to a city named Jerusalem. The people in Jerusalem would not listen. So Aaron went to Ani-Anti. He found Muloki, Ammah, and others already preaching there.

Muloki and Ammah were two of the missionaries who came with the sons of Mosiah to preach to the Lamanites. The Lamanites in Ani-Anti would not listen to Aaron, Muloki, Ammah, or the others.

So Aaron and the missionaries went to Middoni to preach. The Lamanites there did not listen. They put Aaron and a few of the missionaries in prison. The rest of the missionaries ran away and escaped from Middoni.

Aaron, Muloki, and the missionaries in prison were treated very badly. The Lamanites tied them up really tightly with ropes. They didn't give them very much food or water.

When Ammon and king Lamoni came to Middoni, the king of Middoni let Aaron and the other missionaries go. Aaron and his missionaries continued to preach to the Lamanites. This time, many began to believe them.

King Lamoni and Ammon Return

ALMA 21

A mmon and King Lamoni returned to Lamoni's kingdom. King Lamoni told the people they were free from his father, the king of all the Lamanites. Lamoni began to build churches.

King Lamoni also told the people they were free to
worship God how they believed. Ammon began to
preach every day to King Lamoni's people. Ammon
taught them to keep the commandments of God.

Aaron Teaches Lamoni's Father

ALMA 22

Aaron and his companions went to the king of the Lamanites, Lamoni's father. Aaron told the king, "I am Ammon's brother. We have come to be your servants." The king said, "No, you will not be my servants.

I want you to teach me. I don't understand what the Spirit of God is. I don't understand what it means to repent so I can be saved." Aaron said, "Do you believe there is a God?"

"If you say there is, I will believe there is a God. Is He the Great Spirit that led our ancestors out of Jerusalem?" asked the king. "Yes! He created everything," said Aaron.

"Tell me all about the Great Spirit and the creation," said the king. So Aaron began to teach the king about Adam and Eve. He taught the king that God created our bodies to be like His body.

Aaron taught the king that because of the Fall of Adam and Eve, we all need to be saved. Jesus Christ was chosen to save us. Jesus Christ suffered and died so we could be saved. He rose from the dead, so we can live forever.

When Aaron finished teaching, the king asked, "What should I do to be born of God? I want to receive the Spirit so I can be filled with joy! I'll even give up my entire kingdom for this great joy."

"Repent of your sins. Pray to God in faith that you will receive what you asked for," replied Aaron. The king knelt down and put his face down to the ground and began to pray, "God, Aaron told me that you exist.

Will You let me know that You are there? I will give away all my sins to know You. I want to be saved and resurrected someday." As soon as the king finished praying, he fell over as if he had died.

The servants in the room ran to find the queen. They told the queen to come. When the queen arrived, she saw the king on the ground with Aaron standing over him. She thought Aaron had killed the king.

"Kill him!" the queen commanded the servants. But the servants said, "Why are you asking us to kill him? He is stronger than all of us. He could kill all of us." When the queen saw how afraid the servants were, she began to be afraid too.

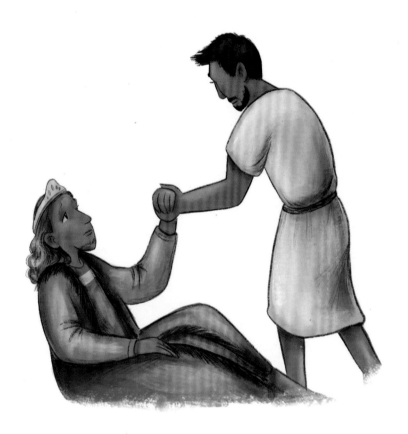

"Then go get the people!" commanded the queen. Aaron bent down and touched the king, "Stand." The king grabbed Aaron's hand and stood up. The queen and the servants who were there were amazed.

Outside, many people began to gather together because of the queen's command. They were angry with Aaron and the missionaries. The king came out and calmed the Lamanites down. He asked Aaron to teach them.

Anti-Nephi-Lehies

ALMA 23–24

The king sent out a command throughout the land. The king commanded his people to not hurt the sons of Mosiah or the other missionaries. He said they should be free to preach to all the Lamanites in the land.

So Aaron, Ammon, Omner, and Himni began to teach the Lamanites. Thousands of Lamanites believed them and were converted. But the Amalekites and Amulonites did not believe and were not converted.

All the Lamanite converts wanted to have a special name they could call themselves. The king and Aaron came up with the name Anti-Nephi-Lehi. So the converts became Anti-Nephi-Lehies and were no longer Lamanites.

The Anti-Nephi-Lehies became a very hard-working people. They were friendly and began to trade with the Nephites. Soon the king grew old. Before he died, he made his son king. His name was Anti-Nephi-Lehi.

King Anti-Nephi-Lehi discovered the Lamanites were preparing to kill them. He spoke to his people, "I thank God He has sent us the sons of Mosiah. I'm thankful to God that He allowed us to repent of our many sins and murders.

Let us not murder anymore. Let us bury our weapons as a testimony to God. Burying our weapons will show God that we have never used them since we repented. If the Lamanites kill us, we will die knowing we are saved."

So the Anti-Nephi-Lehies buried their weapons in a deep pit. They made a covenant with God that they would never kill again. They would rather die than commit sin.

The Lamanites came to fight. The Anti-Nephi-Lehies bowed down and began to pray to God. The Lamanites began to kill them. But the Lamanites soon stopped. They felt guilty killing the helpless Anti-Nephi-Lehies.

The Anti-Nephi-Lehies were not running away. They wouldn't fight either. They were praising God as they were being killed. Over one thousand Anti-Nephi-Lehies died. All of them were righteous.

More than a thousand Lamanites repented and joined the Anti-Nephi-Lehies. The rest of the Lamanites left. The Amalekites and Amulonites lived among the Lamanites. None of them were converted.

Many Lamanites Convert

ALMA 25

The Lamanites were angry with the Nephites. They gathered their armies and began to attack Nephite cities. They started with the city of Ammonihah.

The Lamanites had many battles with the Nephites.
Many of the Lamanites saw how God protected the
Nephites. They began to believe what Aaron and
the sons of Mosiah had taught them.

The Amulonites were the priests of King Noah and their families. Many of them were leaders of the Lamanites. The Amulonites killed the Lamanites who began to believe Aaron's words.

When the other Lamanites heard what the Amulonites had done, they got angry. They hunted the Amulonites down and burned them to death. This fulfilled Abinadi's prophecy that King Noah's priests and families, the Amulonites, would die by fire the way Abinadi had.

The Lamanites returned to their homes. Many of the Lamanites joined the Anti-Nephi-Lehies. They buried their weapons too. They began to have faith in Jesus Christ.

The sons of Mosiah and the missionaries were happy to see how many Lamanites had converted. They were thankful to God for answering their prayers. God had kept His promises to them.

Ammon Glories in the Lord
ALMA 26

Ammon spoke to his brothers. "When we left Zarahemla, we could not have imagined the great blessings God would give us! God blessed us to help thousands of Lamanites become converted to God!

I am full of joy! I know that I could not have done this on my own. I will praise God! With His strength, we can do anything! He has freed so many of the Lamanites from sin and darkness. He has brought them to the light.

God showed us mercy when we tried to destroy His church. He saved us from darkness too. God will show wonderful things to anyone who repents, has faith, and always tries to do good.

Brothers, do you remember when the Nephites laughed at us? They laughed when we told them we were going to preach to the Lamanites. We left hoping we might save a few souls.

We've suffered a lot. The Lamanites have kicked us out of their cities. We have been in prisons. They threw stones at us. They spit on us. They tied us up. They slapped us. But God always comforted us.

We have never seen a people have greater love than the Anti-Nephi-Lehies. They love God and their Lamanite brothers and sisters so much that they would rather die than fight. God cares about all His children!"

Ammon Helps the Anti-Nephi-Lehies Flee

ALMA 27

The Lamanites returned home from losing the war with the Nephites. The Amalekites were especially angry. They caused the Lamanites to be angry with the Anti-Nephi-Lehies. So they began to kill the Anti-Nephi-Lehies again.

Ammon and his brothers went to the king. They told him to help the people escape and join the Nephites. The king said, "If God says we should go, then we will. If not, we will stay here and die."

Ammon prayed to God. God said, "Get them out of the land or they will die. The Anti-Nephi-Lehies are blessed and I will save them." So the Anti-Nephi-Lehies gathered their things and left.

When they were near Zarahemla, they pitched their tents. Ammon and the other sons of Mosiah headed toward Zarahemla. They wanted to ask the chief judge if the Anti-Nephi-Lehies could join the Nephites.

On their way, they met Alma. Together, Ammon, Aaron, Omner, Himni, and Alma went to the chief judge together. The chief judge asked the Nephites if the Anti-Nephi-Lehies could join them. The Nephites said yes and gave them the entire land of Jershon.

The Nephites even sent their army to protect the Anti-Nephi-Lehies. The Nephites wanted them to keep their covenant with God to no longer fight. From then on, the Nephites called the Anti-Nephi-Lehies the people of Ammon.

The Nephites Protect Their People

ALMA 28

The Lamanite army followed the people of Ammon all the way to the land of Jershon. The Nephite army battled the Lamanites. They tried to protect the Nephites and the people of Ammon.

The battle was the worst battle the Nephites and Lamanites had ever had. Thousands of Nephites and Lamanites died. The Nephites were sad. They lost many of their grandfathers, fathers, husbands, and brothers.

The Nephites prayed and fasted for those who died. Because of their faith and hope in Jesus Christ, the Nephites knew their family members were now with God.

Alma Glories in the Lord

ALMA 29

Alma wrote, "I wish I were an angel! I would tell everyone to repent with a voice so strong it would shake the earth! Repent, so there can be less sadness on earth. But I am just a man. I should be okay with what God has given me.

I know God gives us whatever we choose: good or bad. If we choose life or death, or joy or guilt, God will let us have it. I pray God will use me to help others repent. My joy is full when I see someone truly repent.

My joy is even more full because of the success my brothers, the sons of Mosiah, have had with the Lamanites. My joy is so great it feels like my spirit is out of my body! I pray that they will sit someday in God's kingdom. Amen."

Korihor the Anti-Christ

ALMA 30

I n year seventeen of the judges, in the city of Zarahemla, there was a man named Korihor. He did not believe in Jesus Christ. He was an anti-Christ. He even began to teach other Nephites to not believe in Jesus Christ.

Korihor preached, saying, "Why do you believe Jesus Christ will come? Nobody can know the future. How do you know any of it is true? You cannot know what you cannot see. You're all crazy." Many Nephites believed Korihor.

Some Nephites in the city of Gideon did not like what he was teaching. They tied him up and brought him before the high priest and chief judge of Gideon. The high priest and chief judge spoke with Korihor.

Korihor said, "You teach the people about God so you can give them rules and take away their freedom. You say that the words of the prophets are true. I say you have no idea if they're true or if Christ will come.

You say we're all sinners and Jesus Christ will save us from our sins. You tell them God will punish them so you can make yourselves rich and powerful. None of us has seen or heard God—He doesn't exist!"

The high priest and chief judge of Gideon had Korihor tied up and brought to Zarahemla. Korihor was brought before Alma and the chief judge. Alma asked Korihor why he was teaching the people these things.

"Do you believe in God?" asked Alma. "No," replied Korihor. Alma testified, "I know there is a God, and I know someday Jesus Christ will come. Everything around you testifies of God." Korihor replied, "Prove it! Show me a sign of God's power, then I'll believe He exists."

Alma replied, "You have plenty of signs! You have the testimonies of the leaders of the church. You have the scriptures. You have everything on the earth. You even have all the stars in the sky as proof that God exists."

"I won't believe anything unless you show me a sign," said Korihor. "Then here's your sign," said Alma. "In the name of God, you will no longer be able to speak." Immediately, Korihor could no longer speak.

The chief judge gave Korihor something to write with. Korihor wrote, "I cannot speak. I know only God's power could do this to me. I have always known there was a God. Satan tricked me. He appeared to me as an angel.

He told me there was no God. Everything I have taught, he told me. Alma, please pray to God to give my voice back." Alma answered, "God will decide if you get your voice back." But God did not give Korihor his voice back.

The people kicked Korihor out of Zarahemla. News about what happened to Korihor spread quickly. The people who had believed Korihor's teachings repented and returned to the church.

Korihor went to live with some people called Zoramites. He begged them for food and water. One day, he was knocked down and trampled to death. Korihor had followed Satan, and Satan never helps his followers.

Apostate Zoramites

ALMA 31–35

In the land of Antionum lived a group of people called the Zoramites. Alma learned that they had started worshipping idols instead of God. So Alma, Amulek, Zeezrom, Ammon, Aaron, Omner, and two of Alma's sons—Shiblon and Corianton—went to preach to the Zoramites.

When they arrived, they were surprised. The Zoramites had built churches, called synagogues. In the middle of the synagogue, they had built a very tall stand. One at a time, a Zoramite would climb up to the top to pray loudly.

The stand was called the Rameumptom, which means Holy Stand. Each Zoramite who went up would shout the same memorized prayer. Their prayer said that they believed in God but did not believe in Jesus Christ.

Alma prayed for the Zoramites. He prayed that God would bless Alma and the other missionaries to be successful in teaching the Zoramites. Then Alma gave each missionary a blessing. They were each filled with the Holy Ghost.

Alma and his companions began to preach to the Zoramites. While Alma was teaching, a group of poor Zoramites came to ask for help. They wanted to pray in the synagogue, but they were kicked out because they were poor.

Alma said, "I'm glad you have been kicked out. It made you humble. When you are humble, you want to believe and to repent. Some people are stubborn and not humble. They will only believe if someone will show them a sign.

God wants us to have faith. Faith is not knowing, but trusting that something is true even though you cannot see it yet. Seeing a sign isn't faith. Seeing a sign proves God's words are true. You can't believe with faith anymore because you already know.

You cannot know for sure that everything I have taught you is true. So test my words. Have a little faith, even if all you can do is want to believe my words. Then, keep thinking about my words. Over time, you will believe in my words.

Now let's compare the word of God to a seed. Plant these words, like a seed, into your heart and try to believe them. If the seed is good, it will begin to grow. This means if the words are true, you will begin to feel good and understand more. This experience will strengthen your faith.

As you keep planting seeds that are true, you will feel them grow too. When you feel the seed grow, you no longer have faith. Instead you know the truth about those words. You know because you felt the light grow in your heart and your mind understand more.

Now, if the seed doesn't grow, you know those words aren't true, so get rid of them. But you must have faith in the words and think about them long enough for the good seeds to grow. You must take care of the good seeds, so they can grow stronger.

As the good seed grows, you must continue to take care of it so it can grow strong roots. Once the seed grows strong enough, it will grow fruit. It will grow the fruit of the tree of life until you have everlasting life."

The poor Zoramites asked Alma if they should believe in just God. They asked how they can exercise faith in Jesus Christ and plant the seed of faith that Alma had talked about.

Alma replied, "When the Israelites were bitten by snakes, Moses lifted up a serpent on a staff. If they just looked at the serpent on the staff, God would heal them. This was a symbol of God's Son, Jesus Christ.

Look toward Jesus Christ and begin to believe in Him as the Son of God. Plant that word in your heart and feed it with your faith. That seed will grow. Amen."

After Alma finished speaking, Amulek began to teach the poor Zoramites. "I know what Alma has taught you is true. I know that Jesus Christ will die to save us from our sins. Have faith until you repent of your sins.

Pray that God will have mercy on you. Pray in the morning, afternoon, and evening. Pray in your heart for yourself and others around you. But you need to do more than just pray for others, you also need to help them.

So have faith and believe in Jesus Christ. Repent of your sins. Thank God every day in prayer. Pray for help to not sin. Be patient even when you suffer from those who kicked you out of your churches."

When Alma, Amulek, and the other missionaries had finished teaching the Zoramites, they left to the land of Jershon. After they had left, the people began to discuss what they had been taught.

The rich Zoramites were angry with the missionaries because they preached against what they were doing. So the leaders secretly went around to find out who believed what the missionaries had said. Then they kicked the believers out of the city.

Alma helped the Zoramite believers travel to stay with the people of Ammon. The people of Ammon fed them, clothed them, and gave them land to build a new life. Then Alma and his sons returned to Zarahemla.

Alma Counsels His Son Helaman

ALMA 36–37

Alma spoke to his son Helaman, "Listen to me, Helaman. If you keep God's commandments, you will be successful and do well in life. I know God will help whoever trusts Him when they are in trouble."

Alma told Helaman about the time the angel appeared to him and the sons of Mosiah. "I fell down and couldn't move for three days. In those three days, I felt great pain. I knew I had led people away from God.

I remembered all my sins. I knew that I had been fighting against God. I felt horrible. I wanted to disappear and not exist anymore. Then, I remembered something my father had taught me.

My father had taught me about Jesus Christ. Jesus is the Son of God, and He will come to pay for all our sins. So I prayed, "O Jesus, Son of God, have mercy on me." As soon as I had prayed, I didn't feel the pain anymore.

I felt so much joy! My joy was just as strong as my pain had been. Ever since then, I have been teaching people to repent like I did—to feel the same joy I felt. God has blessed me to help many others come to God.

Now, Helaman, take the Nephite records that I have been keeping. I command you to keep a record of the Nephites, like I have done. God will protect them. One day He will let the whole world read and learn from them.

I will teach you something. By small and simple things, God makes large and important things happen. With small methods, God amazes the wise and saves many souls.

God wisely has us keep these records. Our records help the people to remember. They help the people to understand their own mistakes. They help the people to learn about God so they can be saved.

Without the records, the people of Ammon would not have known about God; they couldn't have believed in Jesus Christ as their Savior. God is saving these records for a very important reason. God is trusting you to keep them.

Helaman, preach repentance. Preach faith in Jesus Christ. Teach others to always do good things. Oh, learn to be wise while you are young. Learn to keep the commandments of God while you are young.

Pray to God for help. Let Jesus Christ guide everything you do and think. Ask God for advice in everything, and He will always guide you to do good things.

Now I want to teach you about the Liahona. God made it so Lehi and his family could find their way to the promised land. When Lehi and his family had faith that God would show them the way, then the Liahona worked.

Believing the Liahona would point in the right direction was a small thing. Even though it was small, Lehi's family sometimes still didn't believe, and that's when it would stop working. Helaman, the Liahona is a symbol.

It's as easy for us to listen and obey the words of Jesus Christ as it was for Lehi's family to follow the Liahona. Don't get lazy, Helaman, because of how easy it is to obey God's commandments. Now go preach to the people, my son."

Alma Counsels His Son Corianton

ALMA 38–42

A lma spoke to his other two sons. To Corianton, Alma said, "My son, you have not been keeping God's commandments. When we were teaching the Zoramites, you bragged about how smart and strong you were.

You also left your mission to go after Isabel. She is tempting, but that's no excuse for you. You should have stayed where God trusted you to serve. You should repent.

When the Zoramites saw your behavior, they didn't believe what I was preaching. Follow Jesus Christ again. Don't sin anymore. Go tell the Zoramites you were wrong. Now, let me teach you about the resurrection.

We will all die someday. After we die, we have to wait
to be resurrected. Those who do good in this life
will be happy and at peace while they wait for the
resurrection. But when the wicked die, they will be
sad and afraid.

When it's time, everyone will be resurrected—good and bad. Resurrection is when our body and spirit come back together. Then we will stand before God. He will judge us for what we did during our life.

If you were good in this life, you will return to goodness. If you were evil in this life, you will return to wickedness. The righteous will be restored to endless happiness. The wicked will be restored to endless sadness.

You cannot be restored to something opposite of what you are. In other words, you cannot be wicked and restored to happiness. Wickedness never was happiness.

Now, there are spiritual laws. When we break a spiritual law, that is called sin. We must suffer the punishment for any laws we break. God must punish anyone who breaks the law because He is perfectly just.

God wants to be kind and forgiving, so He created the plan of mercy. Instead of being punished for your sins, Jesus Christ will suffer for any spiritual laws you break. Because of this plan, God can still be perfectly just.

Jesus Christ's suffering for our sins is called the Atonement. When we repent of our sins, God will show us kindness and forgive us. Because of Jesus Christ's Atonement, God can show us mercy, and we can be resurrected.

Corianton, I hope you will repent of your sins so God can forgive you and show you kindness. Now go be a missionary. Teach the people the words of God so they can repent of their sins and have God show them mercy too."

Captain Moroni
Battles Zerahemnah

ALMA 43–44

In year eighteen of the judges, the Zoramites joined the Lamanites. The leader of the Lamanite army was a man named Zerahemnah. Zerahemnah brought his army to battle the Nephites.

The Nephites wanted to protect their wives and their children. They wanted to protect their homes and their freedom to worship God. They knew that if the Lamanites enslaved them, they wouldn't be able to worship God anymore.

The Nephites went to protect themselves and the people of Ammon. The people of Ammon could not fight, but they sent supplies to help the Nephite army. Captain Moroni led the Nephite army.

When the Lamanites came to battle, they became afraid. They saw the Nephites dressed in thick clothes, breastplates, arm-shields, and helmets. So the Lamanites tried to sneak around the Nephites.

God showed Alma where the Lamanites were going. Captain Moroni created a plan. He split his army up and hid them around the city Manti. Then they waited for the Lamanite army to come.

The Lamanites arrived. Captain Moroni's army surprised them. The Nephite army surrounded the Lamanites. The Lamanites died easily because they didn't have armor to protect them.

But after a while, the Nephite army started to lose. Captain Moroni reminded them that they were fighting to protect their families. The Nephites prayed for help. As soon as they prayed, they began to win.

Captain Moroni told Zerahemnah and the Lamanites, "God has protected us. He helped us defeat you. Leave your weapons and promise to never fight Nephites again. If you do, we will let you go home safely. If not, we will destroy you."

Zerahemnah brought his weapons to Captain Moroni. "Here are my weapons. But I will not promise to never fight you again." Captain Moroni replied, "You must promise, or we will continue fighting until you are dead."

Zerahemnah was angry. He picked up his sword to attack Captain Moroni. One of Moroni's soldiers knocked Zerahemnah's sword to the ground. He cut off Zerahemnah's scalp. Zerahemnah ran back to his army.

The battle continued. The Lamanites began to lose again. When Zerahemnah saw they were losing, he shouted to Moroni, "Please let us live, and we promise to never come back."

The Lamanites gave the Nephites their weapons. They promised to never fight Nephites again. Captain Moroni let them leave. The Nephites returned to their homes and families.

Helaman Begins to Keep the Records

ALMA 45

In year nineteen of the judges, Alma came to his son Helaman, "Do you believe in Jesus Christ?" Helaman replied, "Yes, I believe everything you have said." "Write down what I am about to prophesy. But don't share it with anyone," said Alma.

"Jesus Christ will show himself to the Nephites. But four hundred years later, the Nephites will no longer believe. There will be a great war. The Nephites will become Lamanites or be killed. Nephites will no longer exist."

Alma blessed Helaman. Then Alma blessed each of his other sons. Then Alma said, "This land will be cursed to anyone wicked, but it will be blessed to anyone good."

Then Alma left Zarahemla. He was never heard or seen again. He was a righteous man. Many of the Nephites believed that God took him up to heaven the same way God took Moses. Helaman and his brothers began to preach to the Nephites.

Moroni's Title of Liberty

ALMA 46

Many Nephites wouldn't listen to Helaman and his brothers. They were angry with the other Nephites. The leader of this group was a Nephite named Amalickiah. He wanted to be king.

Amalickiah was very smart with his words. He convinced many lower Nephite judges to join him. He promised to make them rulers if they made him king. Even some members of the church believed in Amalickiah.

Captain Moroni heard that Amalickiah was planning to be king. He became angry. He pulled off his cloak and wrote on it. He wrote, "In memory of our God, our religion, and freedom, and our peace, our wives, and our children."

Captain Moroni put on his armor. He tied his cloak to a pole and called it the Title of Liberty. Moroni knelt down and prayed to God. He asked God to protect their freedom as long as there were people who followed and believed in Jesus Christ.

Moroni went out among the Nephites. He waved his title of liberty. He shouted, "Whoever supports what I wrote on this flag, make a promise to God. Protect your rights and religion so God may bless you!"

When the people heard Moroni, they came running with their armor on. They tore off pieces of their clothes. They threw them at Moroni's feet. This was how they made their promise like Moroni had asked.

Moroni and his followers went to many Nephite cities. They raised the title of liberty. They gathered the people together to stand against Amalickiah and his followers.

Soon there were far more people who promised to follow Moroni than Amalickiah. Amalickiah saw that his followers were beginning to doubt and leave him. He decided to go to the land of Nephi with anyone who still believed in him.

Moroni knew that Amalickiah still wanted to be king. He would use the Lamanites to attack the Nephites. So Moroni took the Nephite army and chased Amalickiah. Moroni's army blocked Amalickiah's followers.

Amalickiah and a small group of his men escaped from Moroni's army. The rest of Amalickiah's followers were brought back to Zarahemla. Moroni made Amalickiah's followers promise to support the freedom of the Nephites.

Anyone who refused to promise to support freedom was put to death. Moroni told the people to put the title of liberty on every tower in every Nephite city. The Nephites began to have peace again in the land.

Amalickiah Becomes King of the Lamanites

ALMA 47

Amalickiah and his followers joined the Lamanites. Amalickiah caused many of the Lamanites to be angry with the Nephites. Even the Lamanite king became angry. He commanded the Lamanites to battle the Nephites.

Many of the Lamanites were afraid to battle the Nephites. They ignored the king's command. The king sent Amalickiah with an army to make the scared Lamanites go to battle. Amalickiah took the army.

But Amalickiah wanted to be king. So he made a secret plan. He secretly met with Lehonti, the leader of the scared Lamanites. He told Lehonti to bring his army down in the night and surround Amalickiah's army.

Amalickiah promised to not fight if Lehonti made him the second commander of the whole army. Lehonti agreed. In the morning, when the king's army saw they were surrounded, Amalickiah surrendered.

Lehonti made Amalickiah his second commander. Amalickiah knew if the chief commander died, the second commander became the chief. So Amalickiah had his servant slowly poison Lehonti until he died.

When Lehonti died, the army made Amalickiah their chief commander. Amalickiah returned to the city Nephi where the king of the Lamanites lived. The king was happy to see that Amalickiah had gathered the army.

Amalickiah sent his servants to the king. They killed the king. The king's servants ran away. Amalickiah's servants ran back to the army. They lied to the army. They said the king's servants had killed the king and ran away.

The army chased after the king's servants. They escaped and went to live with the people of Ammon. Amalickiah marched the Lamanite army into the city. He married the queen. Amalickiah's plan had worked. He was now the king of the Lamanites.

Moroni Defends the Nephites

ALMA 48–50

King Amalickiah began to prepare the Lamanites for war. Captain Moroni had also been preparing the Nephites to defend themselves. The Nephites built many walls around their cities and forts to place their armies in.

Captain Moroni and the Nephites were taught to never start a fight. But they were taught to defend themselves, even if it meant they had to kill their enemies. They knew God would protect them if they obeyed His commandments.

At the end of the nineteenth year of the judges, the Lamanites came to battle. They were amazed at the walls the Nephites built to protect themselves. The Nephites had even dug a large ditch around their cities.

The Lamanites tried to attack, but the Nephites were too protected. All the Lamanite captains and over a thousand Lamanites died. But not even one Nephite died. The Nephites thanked God for protecting them.

Amalickiah heard what had happened. He became very angry. He cursed God and promised to kill Moroni. Captain Moroni and the Nephites continued to build protections around their cities.

The Nephites kept God's commandments. They felt safe and happy. At the end of the year, the chief judge, Nephihah, died. He had been a righteous ruler. The Nephites voted and made Nephihah's son, Pahoran, their next chief judge.

King-men vs. Freemen
ALMA 51

In year twenty-five of the judges, some of the richest Nephites wanted to change the law so they could have a king. But Chief Judge Pahoran would not change the law. The Nephites who wanted a king were called king-men.

Everyone who wanted to keep a free government were called freemen. So the Nephites voted. They chose to not change the law and keep a free government. Then Amalickiah returned to battle the Nephites.

The king-men refused to help protect the Nephites from the Lamanites. The people voted to give Captain Moroni the power to force the king-men to fight. The king-men refused and battled Captain Moroni's army instead.

The king-men lost, and Captain Moroni put their leaders in prison. The rest of the king-men chose to fight for Captain Moroni. While Captain Moroni was fighting the king-men, the Lamanite army attacked the city of Moroni and won.

Amalickiah and the Lamanites took many more cities. Each time they took a city, they left Lamanites in the city to protect it. They used the Nephite protections for themselves. Amalickiah sent his army into the land Bountiful.

The Nephite captain Teancum was in Bountiful with his soldiers. They were skillful soldiers. Teancum's army battled all day with Amalickiah's army. When it grew dark, they stopped fighting and set up camp.

When everyone was asleep, Teancum snuck into the Lamanite's camp. He found Amalickiah's tent and stabbed and killed Amalickiah with a spear. Then Teancum snuck back to the Nephite camp.

Bountiful Becomes a Stronghold

ALMA 52–53

In the morning, Teancum's army was ready to battle the Lamanites. The Lamanites found their dead king. They ran back to the city of Mulek to hide. They made Amalickiah's brother, Ammoron, their king.

For two years the Lamanites continued to attack the Nephites. But the Lamanites mostly stayed in their protected cities. The Nephites didn't want to fight them in their cities because it was too difficult.

Captain Moroni, Teancum, and the other chief captains of the Nephites made a plan. They wanted to trick the Lamanites. They wanted them to come out of their cities to battle.

Captain Moroni, Teancum, and another chief captain named Lehi found a way to trick the Lamanites. The Lamanites came out of the city to battle. The Lamanites lost. The Lamanites who didn't die became prisoners.

Teancum made the prisoners build a large ditch around the city Bountiful. The prisoners also built a strong wall of wood at the top of the ditch. The Nephites used Bountiful as a new stronghold to keep their prisoners safe.

The Nephite Prisoners Are Freed

ALMA 54–55

In year twenty-nine of the judges, Ammoron sent Captain Moroni a letter. He asked to exchange prisoners. Moroni told Ammoron he would only trade one Lamanite soldier for one whole Nephite family.

This made Ammoron angry. He wrote back to Moroni. He told Moroni that if the Nephites didn't surrender to the Lamanites, he would destroy them all. Ammoron's letter back to Moroni made Moroni angry.

Moroni decided to help the Nephite prisoners escape instead of exchanging. He knew the Lamanites were guarding the Nephite prisoners in the city of Gid. Moroni sent some of his men with wine to the city of Gid.

When the Lamanite guards saw Moroni's men, they stopped them. Moroni's servant lied to them, saying, "We are Lamanites! We escaped while the Nephites were sleeping. We stole this wine from them too! Enjoy!"

The Lamanite guards drank the wine until they were all drunk and asleep. Moroni's men snuck into the city. They gave the Nephite prisoners weapons, even the women and children. Then Moroni placed his army outside the city.

Moroni could have killed the Lamanites while they slept, but Moroni didn't want to kill anyone if he could. In the morning, when the Lamanites woke up, they saw they were surrounded. So the Lamanites surrendered.

Moroni made the prisoners strengthen the walls and ditches. Then he sent the prisoners to be kept in the stronghold Bountiful.

Helaman and the Two Thousand Stripling Sons

ALMA 53 & 56

Helaman wrote Captain Moroni a letter. "Moroni, the people of Ammon wanted to help fight the Lamanites. They were about to break their oath to God, but their young sons decided to fight so their parents wouldn't have to. They asked me to be their leader.

Two thousand of these young men came with me to Judea to help Antipus defend his city. When the Lamanites saw us arrive, they decided to not attack the city because there were so many of us.

We didn't want to attack the Lamanites either. They were too strong inside their city. We wanted to find a way to get them to come out of their city and attack us. That way, we could defeat them.

We decided to trick the Lamanites. My two thousand sons and I pretended to take supplies to another city. When the Lamanite army saw us leave, they came out of their city and began to chase us. Then Antipus and his army chased them.

When the Lamanites saw they were surrounded, they sped up. They wanted to kill my two thousand sons before they were attacked from behind by Antipus. For three days, they chased us while Antipus chased them.

One morning, the Lamanites weren't chasing us anymore. We thought the Lamanites were trying to trick us to kill us. But we worried that they were attacking Antipus. My sons decided to fight in case Antipus needed our help.

These two thousand young men had never fought before. They were not afraid. They told me their mothers had taught them that if they did not doubt God, He would protect them. They said to me, 'We do not doubt our mothers knew it.'

So we went to attack the Lamanites. When we arrived, we saw that Antipus had reached the Lamanites. The Lamanites were winning, but my two thousand sons fought fiercely. They fought so well that the whole Lamanite army turned around to fight us.

With us attacking them from both sides, the Lamanites were soon defeated. Many of the Lamanites gave themselves up as prisoners.

After the battle, I was afraid many of my sons had been killed. So I gathered them together and counted them. To my great surprise and joy, not a single one of them had been killed! God protected each one!"

The Two Thousand
Stripling Sons Win Again

ALMA 57

Helaman's letter continued. "At the beginning of year twenty-nine of the judges, we received more men and supplies to help us. Sixty more young Ammonite men also came to help. Then the Lamanites came to battle us.

My two-thousand-sixty young sons fought fiercely. They obeyed every command perfectly. I remembered what their mothers had taught them. After the battle, two hundred of them had fainted because they lost so much blood.

All of my young sons had been wounded. But again, not a single one had died! Our whole army was amazed. We knew they had been protected because of their strong faith in God."

The Nephites Win Manti Back
ALMA 58

Helaman continued his letter, "We needed to take the city Manti next, but we didn't have enough soldiers. We sent a letter to Zarahemla asking for more men and food. We didn't receive any for months. We almost starved to death.

After a long time, we got some food and two-thousand men. We didn't have enough soldiers to take Manti, so we made a plan. We sent our army near Manti. Our army was smaller than the Lamanite army.

We hid part of our army. When the Lamanites came out to attack us, we ran away as fast as we could. The Lamanites passed right by our hidden soldiers. The hidden soldiers ran back to the city and took it.

The part of our army that was running away headed toward Zarahemla. The Lamanites were afraid we were leading them into a trap, so they stopped to camp for the night. I had my soldiers march around them in the night.

The next morning, our whole army was safe inside the city Manti. When the Lamanites realized what happened, they returned to their own homes. This is the end of my letter to you, Captain Moroni."

Moroni Sends
Letters to Pahoran

ALMA 59–60

Moroni was so glad for Helaman's successes. He shared their good news. Moroni sent a letter to Chief Judge Pahoran. Moroni asked him to send soldiers and supplies.

The Nephites lost the city of Nephihah to the Lamanites. Moroni and his chief captains began to worry. The Nephites were beginning to be wicked. Moroni knew God would only protect them if they were righteous.

Moroni sent another letter to Pahoran. "You should be sending us supplies and soldiers! Our men have suffered a lot fighting the Lamanites. They have suffered hunger, thirst, and tiredness. Thousands of our soldiers have died.

If you had sent us more supplies and soldiers, fewer soldiers would have died. Their deaths are your fault. You can't sit in your palace and not worry about the Lamanites attacking our people.

You ignored our needs for too long. Do you think God won't punish you for not helping us? If you do not send us soldiers and supplies, then I will come to Zarahemla and kill you."

Pahoran's Letter to Moroni
ALMA 61

M oroni received a letter from Pahoran. "Moroni, I am sorry to hear of your suffering. The king-men have rebelled against me. They have taken over the city of Zarahemla. I am now in the city of Gideon.

The king-men have made Pachus their king.
Pachus is working with Ammoron, the Lamanite
king. Ammoron agreed to make Pachus king over
the Nephites once the Lamanites win the war.

I am building an army to take back Zarahemla. Please help me take back the city. All I want is to protect our people's freedom. Let us fight against evil and find joy in our church, in Christ, and in our God."

King-men Are Destroyed

ALMA 62

After reading Pahoran's letter, Moroni was glad that Pahoran was still faithful. Moroni was sad about the rebellion of the king-men. Moroni took a few men and went to Gideon. He also gathered an army on his way.

Thousands of soldiers came to help fight. They wanted to protect their freedoms. Moroni and Pahoran took their armies to Zarahemla. They battled the king-men. Pachus the king died in the battle.

After the battle, the king-men still alive were put in prison. The law said everyone had to help protect their freedom. Any king-men who refused to fight against the Lamanites was put to death.

The War Ends

ALMA 62

In year thirty-one of the judges, Moroni gathered six thousand soldiers and supplies. He sent them to Helaman and his two chief captains, Lehi and Teancum. Moroni took his own army and left Zarahemla.

Captain Moroni and his army found an army of
Lamanites. He destroyed all but four thousand of
them. The survivors promised to never fight again.
They went and joined the people of Ammon.

Moroni took his army to the city of Nephihah. They camped outside the city. Moroni had his soldiers make ladders and ropes. At night, his army quietly climbed over the walls of the city where the Lamanites weren't watching.

When the Lamanites saw the Nephite army inside the city, they were frightened. They ran out of the city. The Nephites chased them. Many of the Lamanites were captured. They chose to join the people of Ammon.

Moroni, Lehi, and Teancum chased the Lamanites from city to city. Finally, all the Lamanite armies were gathered together in the land of Moroni. Moroni's army surrounded the Lamanites and camped for the night.

Teancum was angry at Ammoron. He blamed Ammoron and his brother Amalickiah for the war that led to so many deaths. Teancum took a rope and snuck over the wall into the Lamanite city at night.

He found king Ammoron and threw a spear at him. The spear didn't kill Ammoron right away. Ammoron shouted for his servants. The servants chased Teancum. They caught and killed Teancum.

Moroni and Lehi were very sad when they found out their friend Teancum had died. They took their army and attacked the Lamanites. They chased the Lamanites completely out of the land. The war was now over.

After the War

ALMA 62–63

The war between the Lamanites and Nephites had lasted many years. Many people had died in the war. Many suffered from hunger. Thanks to the prayers of the righteous, God had saved the Nephites.

Because of the horrible sufferings during the war, many Nephites became hardened. They became cold-hearted and chose to not feel anymore.

But many other Nephites turned to God because of their sufferings. Instead of hardening their hearts, they opened their hearts to God.

Captain Moroni immediately began to strengthen the weakest parts of the land. When he finished, he gave his son Moronihah command of the army. Moroni then returned to Zarahemla and retired in peace.

Helaman went back to preaching the gospel. Many believed in his words and were baptized. Pahoran returned to the judgment seat. The Nephites elected more judges who managed the laws.

The Nephites began to be rich again, but they did not become prideful this time. They remembered God and kept His commandments. In year thirty-five of the judges, Helaman died.

After Helaman died, the records went to his brother, Shiblon. Moroni died in year thirty-six of the judges. Shiblon died later in year thirty-nine of the judges. Before Shiblon died, he gave the records to Helaman's son, who was also called Helaman.

About the Author and Illustrator

AUTHOR

Jason Zippro holds a master's degree in education from the University of Missouri-Saint Louis, a master's degree in business administration from the University of Utah, and a bachelor of arts degree in Italian with a minor in editing from Brigham Young University. Jason worked as an editor for four years before teaching eighth-grade English for three years in Kansas City with the non-profit Teach for America. Jason and his wife, Sharolee, have four young children.

ILLUSTRATOR

Alycia Pace graduated from Brigham Young University with a bachelor of fine arts degree in animation and is a freelance illustrator from her home in Utah. She has written and illustrated several books including *Polly the Perfectly Polite Pig* (available at Deseret Book and Barnes & Noble) and *How to Potty Train a Dinosaur.* She loves the smell of bookstores and exploring new places with her two children and adventurous husband.

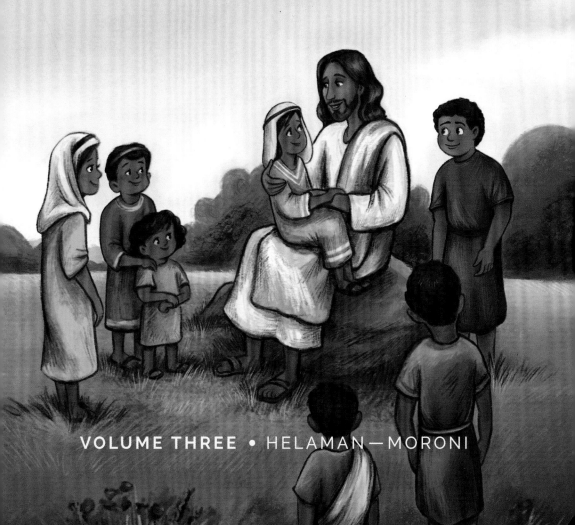

BOOK OF MORMON
STORIES *for* KIDS

VOLUME THREE • HELAMAN—MORONI

This book belongs to:

_____

BOOK OF MORMON

STORIES for KIDS

VOLUME THREE • HELAMAN—MORONI

Text adapted by Jason Zippro
Illustrated by Alycia Pace

ISBN 13: 978-1-7349053-4-2

REL046000 RELIGION / Christianity / Church of Jesus Christ of Latter-day Saints (Mormon)
REL091000 RELIGION / Christian Education / Children & Youth
JNF049200 JUVENILE NONFICTION / Religious / Christian / Early Readers

Cover design © 2021 Primary Scriptures, LLC
Illustrations by Alycia Pace
Cover design by Angela Baxter
Edited and typeset by Emily Chambers and Kaitlin Barwick

Distributed by

CEDAR FORT
Publishing & Media

10 9 8 7 6 5 4 3 2 1

www.PrimaryScriptures.com

CONTENTS

HELAMAN

Pahoran, Pacumeni, and Paanchi

HELAMAN 1

In year forty of the judges, Chief Judge Pahoran died. Pahoran had three sons who wanted to be chief judge. His son who was also called Pahoran won the people's vote. But Pahoran's brother Paanchi wanted to be chief judge instead.

Before Paanchi could get his followers to help him take over, he was put in prison. He was sentenced to die for trying to destroy the freedom of the Nephites. Paanchi's followers were angry. They made a plan to save him.

Paanchi's followers picked a man named Kishkumen to kill Pahoran. Kishkumen put on a disguise and then snuck in and killed Pahoran on the judgment seat. He ran away so fast that he wasn't caught.

Kishkumen later returned. He and the other followers made a secret promise to never tell what happened. The Nephites voted for Pahoran's brother Pacumeni to be their new chief judge. That was the end of year forty of the judges.

The Nephites were so busy with Pahoran, Pacumeni, and Paanchi that they didn't see a large Lamanite army coming to battle Zarahemla. The Nephites didn't have time to gather their army. The Lamanites came right into the city and killed Pacumeni.

Coriantumr, the captain of the Lamanite army, thought he could take all the Nephite cities as easily as he took Zarahemla. So he took his army to attack the city Bountiful.

Moronihah took the Nephite armies and surrounded
Coriantumr. The armies fought. Coriantumr died in
the battle. Moronihah sent the rest of the Lamanites
back home.

Kishkumen and Gadianton

In year forty-two of the judges, the Nephites voted for Helaman to be their chief judge. The leader of Kishkumen and the rest of Paanchi's followers was a man named Gadianton. He wanted to be chief judge.

Gadianton asked Kishkumen to kill Helaman. One of Helaman's servants found out about the secret group. He gave Kishkumen a secret hand sign. Kishkumen thought Helaman's servant was one of his secret group.

Kishkumen told Helaman's servant what he was going to do. When Helaman's servant found out, he stabbed Kishkumen in the heart. He went and told Helaman what had happened. Helaman sent soldiers to capture the secret group.

But when Kishkumen didn't make it back, Gadianton became worried. He gathered his secret group. They snuck out of the city through a secret passageway. When the soldiers came, there was no one left to arrest.

Helaman Is Chief Judge

HELAMAN 3

Helaman was a just chief judge. He followed God's commandments. The Nephites had peace for several years. But after awhile, the Nephites began to argue with each other. Many decided to leave and start their own cities.

Helaman had two sons. He named the older son Nephi and the younger one Lehi. In year forty-nine of the judges, tens of thousands of people joined the church. God also blessed the members to become very rich.

In year fifty-one of the judges, some members of the church began to think they were better because they were richer. Their pride got even worse over the next few years.

In year fifty-three of the judges, Helaman died. The people voted Helaman's son Nephi to be their chief judge. Nephi was a good ruler. He kept the commandments of God, just like his father.

Nephite Wickedness and the Loss of Zarahemla

HELAMAN 4

The Nephites became even more prideful. They ignored God's commandments. The Nephites didn't help the poor or needy. They began to lie, steal, and cheat. They stopped believing in revelation.

The Nephites began to argue with each other. They got so angry with each other that they fought. Many Nephites died. Other Nephites left to live with the Lamanites. They were called dissenters.

The Nephite dissenters made the Lamanites angry with the Nephites. The Lamanites and Nephite dissenters attacked the Nephites. The Nephites lost many cities, even their capital city Zarahamela.

Captain Moronihah, Nephi, and Lehi preached to the Nephites. Some Nephites began to remember the teachings of Alma, Mosiah, and other prophets. As they began to repent, they began to win more battles.

The Nephites were very outnumbered. They were only able to get back half of their cities. The Nephites lived in fear. They were afraid that the Lamanites would take over all their lands.

Nephi and Lehi in Prison

HELAMAN 5

In year sixty-two of the judges, Nephi chose to no longer be chief judge. A man named Cezoram became chief judge. Most Nephites were not righteous. Nephi and Lehi decided to preach repentance.

When Nephi and Lehi were young, their father Helaman taught them. He taught, "You must build your life on Jesus Christ. He is like a rock you build a house on. When storms come, the house stays sturdy and strong."

Nephi and Lehi taught in all the Nephite cities. Then they went to the Lamanite cities to teach them too. The Lamanite army caught them and put them in prison.

The Lamanites kept Nephi and Lehi in prison for many days. One day, a group of Lamanites came to kill Nephi and Lehi. When they arrived, Nephi and Lehi were surrounded by fire. But they were not burned. The Lamanites did not dare touch them.

Nephi and Lehi spoke to the Lamanites, "Do not be afraid. God is doing this so you cannot kill us." Then the prison and earth shook. Darkness filled the prison so no one could see. The Lamanites were afraid.

They heard a calm, strong voice say, "Repent! Do not try to kill my servants anymore!" In the prison was a Nephite who had joined the Lamanites. He looked and saw Nephi and Lehi glowing in the darkness.

This Nephite's name was Aminadab. He told the Lamanites to look. "What does this mean?" asked the Lamanites. "You must repent and have faith in Jesus Christ. Then the darkness will disappear," said Aminadab.

The Lamanites began to pray to God. The darkness went away. When the darkness left, they saw that all three hundred people in the prison were surrounded by fire. None of the Lamanites were burned.

The Lamanites felt peaceful and happy. They heard the voice of God, "Because of your faith in Jesus Christ, you will be at peace." The Lamanites looked up. They saw angels come out of heaven. The angels taught them many things.

Everyone in prison went out and taught the Lamanites about what had happened. Many of the Lamanites believed. Many of the Lamanites gave up fighting. The Lamanites gave back many of the cities they took from the Nephites.

Gadianton Robbers Take Over the Government

HELAMAN 6

In year sixty-three of the judges, most of the Lamanites were more righteous than the Nephites. Many Lamanites went to Zarahemla and the land north to preach. Nephi and Lehi joined them as missionaries.

In year sixty-four of the judges, there was peace between the Nephites and Lamanites. Anyone could travel wherever they wanted. They traded with each other. They soon became a very rich people.

In year sixty-six of the judges, chief judge Cezoram
was secretly killed. His son was voted as chief judge,
but he was also killed. Gadianton's followers had
murdered them. They did it in secret, so no one
knew who did it.

Gadianton's group did everything secretly. They had secret signs and words so they knew who was in their group. They secretly stole from others. They even murdered others. They followed Satan instead of God.

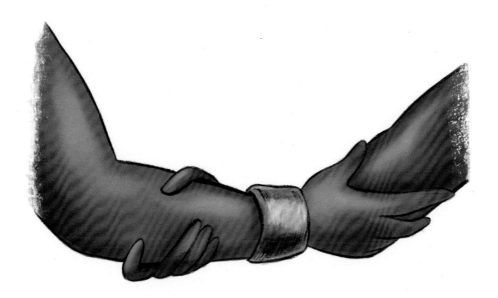

Over the next several years, more and more Nephites became Gadianton robbers. The Lamanites became stronger followers of God. They tried to destroy the robbers.

By the end of year sixty-eight of the judges, the Gadianton robbers were even in control of the Nephite government.

Nephi Prays on His Garden Tower

HELAMAN 7–9

In year seventy-one of the judges, Nephi went home to Zarahemla after preaching to the Nephites in the north. Many judges were now Gadianton robbers. The judges weren't just. Instead, they punished the righteous.

Nephi was very sad and frustrated. He went onto his garden tower to pray to God. "I wish I lived at a different time, but I live now among the wicked Nephites. I am so sad because of how wicked the Nephites are."

Nephi's garden tower was next to the main road to the market in Zarahemla. People traveling to the market overheard Nephi. They gathered outside his garden wall to listen. When Nephi stood up, he saw them.

"Why have you all gathered? So you can listen to me tell you of how wicked you are? Repent! You have stopped listening to God so that you can focus on getting famous and rich. You steal, lie, and kill each other.

You let the Gadianton robbers rule the city! If you do not repent, you will be destroyed!" A few people in the crowd were secretly Gadianton robbers. They were angry with Nephi. They said, "Why do you let Nephi speak to us this way? Take him, so he can be judged!"

The robbers didn't take Nephi though. They were afraid the people would be angry with them because some people believed Nephi. These people said, "Leave Nephi alone! He is a good man, and what he says is true. We should repent!"

Nephi continued to teach the people. He taught them about prophets. He taught them that prophets warn the people to repent before they're destroyed. If the people do not listen to the prophets, then they will be destroyed.

Nephi continued, "You are becoming very wicked. You will soon be destroyed. Even now your chief judge is dead. He was killed by his brother who wants to be chief judge. Both of them are Gadianton robbers!"

Five men listening to Nephi ran to see if what Nephi said was true. When they arrived at the judgment seat, they saw the chief judge dead on the floor. They were so shocked that they fell over on the ground.

The people arrested them because they thought the five men had killed the chief judge. They also arrested Nephi. Some judges thought Nephi helped the killer because he knew the chief judge had died.

Nephi spoke to the judges. "You fools. Chief Judge Seezoram was killed by his brother Seantum. Go to Seantum's house. Ask him if he killed his brother and if I helped him. He will tell you no and pretend to be surprised.

Then look at his clothes. You will find blood on them. Ask him where the blood came from. He will be nervous. Then he will confess to killing his brother. Then you will know I am a prophet sent from God."

The people did as Nephi said. Everything happened just the way Nephi said it would. So they freed the five men and Nephi. Many people believed Nephi was a prophet.

Nephi Receives God's Blessing

HELAMAN 10–12

Nephi started walking home after the people let him free. He thought about how wicked the people were becoming. It made him very sad. Then Nephi heard God's voice saying, "Bless you, Nephi!

You have tried to always follow me and to keep my commandments. You are Nephi, and I am God. I know you will never ask me for anything that I wouldn't want. So anything you ask for, I will give you. Go and tell the people to repent!"

Nephi immediately turned around and went back to preach to the people. Many people were angry with his message. They tried to put him in prison. The Spirit helped Nephi to escape before they could grab him.

For the rest of the year, Nephi preached repentance until everyone had heard his message. But the Nephites would not listen. They even began to fight and kill each other.

For the next two years, Nephi saw the people die in war. Nephi asked God to not let their food grow, so they would grow hungry. Nephi hoped they would stop fighting and remember God if they were hungry.

God did as Nephi asked. Their food dried up and wouldn't grow. They became very hungry. Thousands of people died from hunger. They started to remember God. They asked Nephi to pray to God for help.

Nephi prayed to God because the people had repented. God listened and let their food grow again. The Nephites were good for only a few years. Soon they became wicked again. Many people joined the Gadianton robbers.

Samuel the Lamanite Preaches

HELAMAN 13–16

In year eighty-six of the judges, the Nephites were very wicked. But the Lamanites were righteous. There was one Lamanite named Samuel who came to Zarahemla to preach to the wicked Nephites. The Nephites threw him out of the city.

Samuel began to leave, but then God told him to return to Zarahemla to preach. The Nephites wouldn't let Samuel back into the city. So Samuel climbed up the outer wall of the city. He stood on the wall and began to preach.

"I am Samuel, a Lamanite. God has told me to warn you. You will be destroyed if you do not repent! God has only saved this great city of Zarahemla because of the righteous living here. God will save you if you repent.

You care about your riches more than anything else.
So God has placed a curse on this land. A curse where
you will lose your riches. Now I give you a sign. In five
more years, there will be a day and a night and a day
without darkness.

This will be the sign that Jesus Christ will be born the next day. A new star will appear in the sky. Many of you will fall to the earth from surprise. God has commanded me to tell you these things.

We know that Jesus Christ must die, so that we can someday be resurrected. He must die so we can be saved from our sins and return to live with God in heaven. So I will give you another sign.

This will be the sign of His death. The sun, moon, and stars will go dark. There will be no light in the land from when Jesus dies until He rises from the dead three days later. There will also be lightning and thunder.

The earth will shake and crack. Rocks will break. There will be great wind storms. Roads and cities will be destroyed. These things will happen for several hours. Then darkness will cover the land for three days.

Remember, you are free to choose good or evil. God has blessed you to know the difference between good and evil. You can choose to do good and have eternal life, or you can choose to do evil and die. So repent!"

Many Nephites heard Samuel speak from the wall. Many of them believed him. They went to find Nephi. They repented of their sins and Nephi baptized them. But many did not believe Samuel. They were angry with him.

Some angry Nephites took stones and threw them at Samuel. Others shot arrows. God protected Samuel. None of their stones or arrows could hit him. This made more Nephites believe Samuel the Lamanite.

Most of the Nephites did not believe Samuel. When they saw that they couldn't hit him, they decided to catch him and tie him up. Before they could get him, Samuel jumped down from the wall and escaped.

For the next few years, the Nephites grew more wicked. There were only a few righteous Nephites. Angels visited some of them. God even sent great signs like the prophets had said, but most of the Nephites didn't believe them.

3RD & 4TH NEPHI

The Sign of Jesus Christ's Birth

3 NEPHI 1

Nephi the prophet gave all the Nephite records to his son. Nephi traveled out of the land and was never seen or heard from again.

Nephi's son was also named Nephi. He began to write down what happened to the people in his day. He wrote that many of the signs and miracles the prophets spoke about began to come true.

Many Nephites didn't believe the prophecies. They said Samuel's sign would've happened by now if it were true. The unbelievers decided to kill all the believers if the sign didn't happen by a certain day.

The believers began to worry the sign wouldn't happen in time. But they trusted Samuel's prophecy and watched for the sign. They waited for the night that would be as bright as day.

When Nephi learned what the unbelievers planned to do, he prayed to God for help. Christ spoke to him, "Nephi, be calm and don't worry. Tomorrow I will be born. So tonight the sign will be given."

That night the sun went down, but the night sky didn't get dark. Everyone was amazed. Many unbelievers fell to the ground because they were so shocked. What Samuel the prophet had said did come true!

As prophesied, a new star appeared in the sky. In the morning, the sun came up like it normally did. Many unbelievers began to believe and repent of their sins. So, Nephi baptized them. And there was peace again.

Lachoneus Defends against the Robbers

Satan began to trick the people. He made the people think the signs didn't happen. He made them think the signs were made-up stories. Many people began to not believe in the signs anymore.

The people began to be very wicked again. They ignored the teachings of the prophets. Many of the Nephites and Lamanites began to join the robbers who lived in the mountains.

The robbers continued to cause trouble. The Nephites and Lamanites gathered together to protect themselves. Thirteen years after Samuel's sign of Christ's birth, a war began against the robbers.

The ruler of the robbers was a man named Giddianhi. He was a wicked man. The ruler of the Nephites and Lamanites was a man named Lachoneus. He was a good man who believed in God.

Giddianhi sent Lachoneus a letter. Giddianhi told Lachoneus they should give up and join the robbers. Giddianhi would command his people to kill all the Nephites and Lamanites if they didn't.

Lachoneus was not afraid. He told his people to repent and pray to God for strength. God would not let the robbers destroy them if they prayed and repented. All the people obeyed Lachoneus.

Lachoneus commanded his people to gather between the cities Zarahemla and Bountiful. Thousands of people came with their families and animals.

Lachoneus had the people prepare for war. He commanded the people to build walls all around to protect them. He sent guards to watch for the robbers day and night. They made weapons, armor, and shields.

Lachoneus organized the Nephite and Lamanite armies. He chose people with the spirit of prophecy to be captains over the armies. The Chief Captain over the entire army was Gidgiddoni.

Gidgiddoni was a great prophet. The people asked him to attack the robbers first. Gidgiddoni refused. He said if they waited for the robbers to attack first, God would help the Nephites and Lamanites to win.

The Nephites Defeat the Robbers
3 NEPHI 4

A few months later, the robbers came to battle the Nephites. The robbers thought the Nephites were afraid because they were kneeling. But the Nephites were praying to God for strength.

The robbers and Nephites battled very hard. It was the worst battle the Nephites ever had. When the robbers began to lose, they ran away. Gidgiddoni commanded his army to chase the robbers.

Giddianhi, the leader of the robbers, tried to run away too. He was tired from the battle. The Nephites caught up to him and killed him. The robbers didn't come back for almost two years.

When the robbers returned, they surrounded the city. They wanted to trap the Nephites inside. They hoped the Nephites would run out of food. But the Nephites had enough food storage for seven years.

The robbers did not have food storage. They could only hunt wild animals. The robbers soon ran out of food and began to starve. Their new leader, Zemnarihah, decided to give up and leave.

Gidgiddoni made a plan to defeat the robbers as they were leaving. He knew the robbers were weak because they were hungry. So Gidgiddoni snuck half his army out of the city at night and waited.

When the robbers began to leave, Gidgiddoni's army chased the robbers. The robbers tried to run away, but the army hiding outside of the city blocked them. The Nephites surrounded and trapped the robbers.

Zemnarihah and many robbers were destroyed. But some robbers gave up and became prisoners. The Nephites thanked God. They knew God had protected them from the robbers because they had repented.

The Nephites Repent and Preach

3 NEPHI 5

All of the Nephites believed the prophets. They saw many signs. They knew the signs meant Christ had been born on the earth. Everyone repented of their sins. They eagerly served God day and night.

The Nephites sent missionaries to teach the robbers
in prison. Some robbers promised to never kill again.
The Nephites let those robbers go free.

Many wonderful things happened to the people over the next several years. There were so many good things that happened to them that Nephi couldn't write them all down.

Mormon Writes the History of the Nephites

3 NEPHI 5

Years later, the prophet Mormon took the records of the Nephites. Mormon wrote down many Nephite stories in the Gold Plates.

Mormon wrote, "I am a follower of Jesus Christ. He asked me to share His words. He wants all of us to live with God. That is why I wrote this record. It tells what happened to the Nephites and Lamanites.

Heavenly Father and Jesus Christ have given us so much knowledge. They have taught my people how to be saved and live with Them again. Whenever my people obeyed God, He has blessed them.

Someday God will gather His children again from all over the world. He will help them learn the promises He has made with them. And all His children will know their Redeemer, Jesus Christ."

The Nephites Grow Rich and Wicked
3 NEPHI 6

The Nephites began to spread out over the land. They used their food storage to help start their lives again. The Nephites rebuilt many of their cities.

The Nephites gave any robbers who repented a place to live. Lachoneus, Gidgiddoni, and the other great leaders made new laws. The laws were equal and fair to everyone. The new laws kept peace and order.

Some Nephites began to make more money than others. Satan made the rich Nephites think that they were better because they were richer.

Over nine years the people became very wicked, even the members of the church. Everyone knew God's commandments, but they chose to disobey them. They cared more about being rich and powerful.

God began to send prophets to the Nephites. They taught about Jesus Christ. They told the people to repent. Many people became angry with the prophets, but the judges and lawyers were the most angry.

Secretly, some judges killed a few prophets. When the Chief Governor found out, he brought the judges to Zarahemla. They needed to be punished for killing the prophets.

Many of the other lawyers and judges wanted to protect the judges who killed the prophets. They made a secret society. They decided to kill the Chief Governor and make one of them the king.

The Nephites Break Apart into Tribes
3 NEPHI 7

The leader of the secret society was a man named Jacob. The secret society killed the Chief Governor, hoping to make Jacob king instead. But when the Chief Governor died, the people split into many tribes.

Each tribe chose their own chief to lead them. All the tribes agreed to not fight each other. But all the tribes hated Jacob's tribe because they had killed the Chief Governor. So Jacob's tribe ran away to safety.

Even though the people agreed to not fight each other, they were still wicked. They threw stones at the prophets and kicked them out of their cities. So Nephi began to preach to the people too.

Nephi told the people to repent. He was filled with the Spirit. Angels came down from heaven and visited him every day. He preached the gospel. Anyone who heard him knew what he was saying was true.

Even though people knew what Nephi said was true, they still didn't change. Many were angry with Nephi because he was so powerful. He cast out evil spirits and even raised his brother from the dead.

Nephi continued to teach the people for more than a year. Very few people repented of their sins. Those who did repent were baptized. But most of the Nephites stayed wicked.

The Signs of Jesus Christ's Death

3 NEPHI 8

Thirty-three years passed since Samuel's sign of a day and a night and a day without any darkness. The people began to look for Samuel's other sign where there would be three days of darkness.

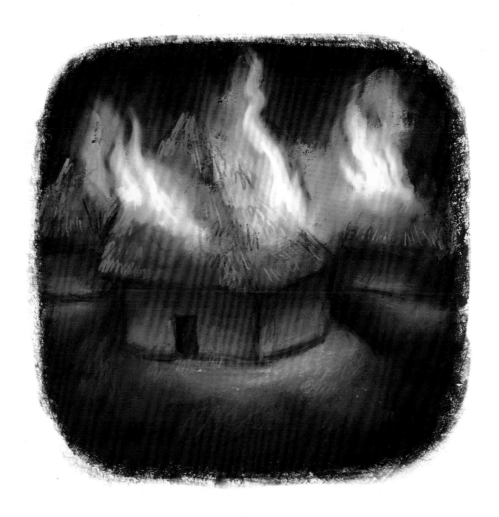

In the first month of the thirty-fourth year, there was the greatest storm the Nephites had ever seen. There was thunder and lightning. Many cities caught fire. Even the great city of Zarahemla burned.

There were tornadoes, and it poured rain. Every single city was damaged or destroyed. And many cities sank into the sea, like the city of Moroni.

Earthquakes shook the cities. The roads between the cities broke apart. Rocks cracked, and the ground split open. Several cities were buried, like the city of Moronihah.

All these terrible things happened over three hours. Many people died. When the storms finished, a thick, dark fog covered the land. It blocked out the sun. No one could even light a fire to see.

The darkness lasted three days, just as Samuel had prophesied. During that time, the earth continued to shake. The people wished they had repented sooner. They were sad for those who died in the storms.

Jesus Christ Speaks to the Nephites from Heaven

3 NEPHI 9

On the third day, the people heard a voice. "Beware, my people! Many of my sons and daughters have died because they did not repent. They did not listen to the prophets, but killed them instead.

I burned many cities and the people in them. I sank many cities into the sea and the people in them. And I buried many cities and the people in them. I did this because they were wicked and did not repent.

I saved all of you. You were more righteous than those who died. Will you now come to me and repent, so I can heal you? If you come to me, I will show you kindness and love. I will give you eternal life.

I am Jesus Christ, the Son of God. I created the heavens and the earth. I am the Light and Life of the World. Believe in me. Show me you're sorry for your sins. Repent and I will give you the Holy Ghost. I died and came back to life so you can live with God again. So repent and be saved."

Prophets Always Warn the People before Destruction

3 NEPHI 10

All the people were amazed! They stopped crying and were silent. They listened to the voice again, "Oh my people! I tried to gather you like a hen gathers her baby chicks, but you would not come."

Then the earth stopped shaking. The cracks in the ground shut again. The darkness went away. The people began to thank Jesus Christ. They began to be joyful again.

Moroni explained that the prophets had warned about the fires, storms, earthquakes, and signs of darkness. But many of the people did not believe and had killed the prophets for warning them.

Moroni warned, "If you have the scriptures, study them. Read and try to understand them. The prophets write scriptures. The things they write down are to help us be good, and warn us about what will happen."

Jesus Christ Descends from Heaven

3 NEPHI 11

In the city of Bountiful, many people gathered near the temple. They were talking about Jesus Christ. While they were speaking they heard a voice. They did not understand what the voice said.

The voice was soft and gentle, but it caused their hearts to burn. The people heard the voice a second time. They still did not understand. They looked up at the sky where the voice came from.

The third time they heard the voice, they listened and understood. The voice said, "Look! This is my beloved Son. I am pleased with Him. He has honored my name. Listen to Him!"

The people silently watched as a man came down out of heaven. He said, "I am Jesus Christ. The prophets testified I would come. I am the Light of the World. I have taken everyone's sins upon me."

All the people knelt and bowed to Jesus Christ. He said, "Stand and come to me. Feel the marks in my hands, feet, and side. Then you will know I am the Savior of the world. I died to save you all from sin."

The people went one by one to feel the marks on Christ's body. When every person finished, they all shouted, "Hosanna! Blessed be the name of the Most High God!" And they all bowed at Christ's feet.

Then Jesus said, "Nephi, come to me." Nephi came, bowed down, and kissed Jesus's feet. Then Jesus called others to Him. He gave twelve of them the power to baptize.

Jesus Christ Teaches How To Baptize

3 NEPHI 11–12

Jesus Christ taught the twelve how someone should be baptized. "If someone repents of their sins and wants to be baptized, then you can baptize them.

Stand in some water. Then say, 'Having authority given me of Jesus Christ, I baptize you in the name of the Father, and of the Son, and of the Holy Ghost. Amen.'

Then lower them underneath the water until their whole body is covered. Then help them up out of the water. This is how you should baptize.

Repent of your sins. Be baptized in the way I just showed you. Then continue to believe and trust me like small children do. If you do these things, then you will be saved. You will live in heaven again someday."

Then Jesus told the people, "I have chosen these twelve. You will be blessed if you listen and obey them. I have given them power to baptize you. Then you will receive the Holy Ghost, and your sins will be forgiven."

Jesus Christ Speaks the Beatitudes

3 NEPHI 12

Jesus blessed the people saying, "Those who are humble will be blessed to live in God's kingdom. Those who are sad and suffering will be blessed with comfort.

Those who are gentle and patient will be blessed to enjoy all good things. Those who try to do right things will be blessed with the Holy Ghost. Those who are kind and forgiving will be blessed with forgiveness.

Those whose hearts are focused on God will be blessed to someday see God. Those who help others be calm and kind will be called the children of God.

Those who are hurt by others because they chose to follow me, will be blessed to live happily in God's kingdom. Remember that even the prophets before you were hurt for following me."

Jesus Christ Commands Us To Obey a Higher Law

3 NEPHI 12

J esus taught the people to be good examples to the world. "You are like salt. When you add salt to food, it makes it taste better. You are also like a city on a mountain top—it can be seen from everywhere.

If you light a candle, do you hide it? No, you use it to shine light so you can see. When you do good things, you are like a light for other people.

You've been commanded to not kill. But I say, don't even get angry with others. Find a way to help everyone be happy and agree. Try to do this even with people you don't like.

When you get married, be loyal to your spouse. Be loyal not only in everything you do, but also in everything you think.

If someone asks you to do something, say, 'Yes, I will do that' or 'No, I can't do that.' If you say you're going to do something, do it.

Care about and forgive others. Love everyone—even your enemies. If they try to do or say mean things to you, pray for them. Don't try to get even. Always be kind in return.

If you really seek to do good, as if you are hungry for it, then you will be filled with the Holy Ghost. I want you to be perfect like me and Heavenly Father. I have taught you these things to help you be perfect too."

Jesus Christ Teaches about Prayer and Prophets

3 NEPHI 13–14

Jesus taught the people to pray: "'Our Father in heaven, holy is Your name. May Your purposes be done on earth as they are in heaven. Forgive us, as we forgive others.

Help us not want to do bad things. Save us from evil. It is Your kingdom, power, and greatness that will last forever. Amen.'

Choose things that will give you blessings in heaven. Don't focus on things that will only make you rich on earth. Choosing spiritual things will fill you with light. What you focus on is what you care about most.

Ask for what you need, and God will give it to you. Look for what is good, and God will help you find it. Knock on God's door to enter, and He will open it and let you in.

Remember that the path to evil is large and wide. It is easy to follow. There will be many people that follow it. The path to heaven is narrow. There will be very few that follow it.

Follow true prophets. You will know if they are true by what they do. They are like fruit trees. If the tree is a bad tree, the fruit will be bad. But only a good fruit tree can make good fruit.

If you do what I say, you are like a wise man who builds his house on a rock. When it rains, his house will not fall. But a foolish man builds his house on sand. When it rains, his house will wash away."

Jesus Christ Has Many Sheep

3 NEPHI 15–16

Jesus continued to teach the people, "Do not be surprised when I say the old way is done. Now there is a new way. I am the one who gave you the old way, called the Law of Moses. That law is now finished.

I told the people in Jerusalem that I am the shepherd. I told them that I have other sheep that are not in Jerusalem. You are some of the sheep that I was talking about. And there are still other sheep I must visit.

The new way is called the gospel. In the last days, I will bring my gospel to all my sheep. My sheep are called the House of Israel. Everyone else is called a Gentile. I will also bring my gospel to them."

Jesus Christ Heals the People and Blesses the Children

3 NEPHI 17

Jesus needed to visit other people besides the Nephites. He looked and saw the people watching Him with tears in their eyes. They wished Jesus would stay. So, Jesus decided to stay a little longer.

Jesus said, "Bring anyone who is sick, blind, or deaf. Bring anyone who cannot walk or speak or has any issue. If you bring them to me, I will heal them." So they brought their sick, and He healed them all.

Jesus asked them to bring their small children to Him. They sat the children on the ground all around Him. Jesus asked the adults to kneel down. Jesus knelt down too and prayed for the children.

Jesus said wonderful things in His prayer. They were so wonderful that they could not write them down. Jesus said, "You are blessed because of your faith. I am full of joy." Then He cried with happiness.

Jesus blessed each child one by one. He prayed for each child. He cried again with happiness. He told the parents, "Look at your children!"

When the parents looked, heaven opened up. Angels came down and circled around the children. It looked like they were surrounded by fire. The angels taught and helped the children.

Jesus Christ Teaches
about the Sacrament
3 NEPHI 18

Jesus told the twelve disciples to get bread and wine. Jesus broke the bread in pieces and blessed it. He gave it to the disciples. They ate the bread. Then the disciples gave everyone else the bread to eat too.

Jesus taught, "Do this to remember my body, which I have shown to you. Eating this bread will show that you always remember me. If you always remember me, then you will have my Spirit to be with you."

Jesus took the wine and blessed it. He gave it to the disciples to drink. Then the disciples gave everyone else the wine to drink too. Jesus taught, "Drink this wine to remember my blood, which I shed for you.

Drinking this wine will show Heavenly Father you want to obey my commandments. I command everyone who is baptized to eat this bread and drink this wine. If you obey, you will be blessed."

Jesus continued to teach the people, "Pray always
to protect yourself from Satan. He will always try to
tempt you because he wants you to fail like he has.
Pray for your families so they will be blessed.

God will give you every good thing you ask for. So meet and pray together in church often. Pray for each other, even those who aren't at church. Follow my example, and you will be a light to the world."

After Jesus said these things, He gave each of the twelve disciples the power to give the Gift of the Holy Ghost. Then a cloud came down and carried Jesus into heaven.

The Nephite Disciples Teach and Are Baptized

3 NEPHI 19

The people left and told their family and friends they had seen Jesus. They said He would come again. So many people traveled all night to Bountiful so they could see Jesus the next day.

Now the twelve disciples were Nephi; his brother Timothy, who Nephi raised from the dead; Nephi's son Jonas; Mathoni; Mathoni's brother, Mathonihah; Kumen; Kumenonhi; Jeremiah; Shemnon; Jonas; Zedekiah; and Isaiah.

The people gathered around the temple. The twelve disciples separated them into twelve groups. Each disciple took a group and taught them what Jesus had taught. They knelt down and prayed together.

Then everyone walked to the water. Nephi got in and was baptized first. Then Nephi baptized the other eleven disciples. Then they received the Holy Ghost. Heaven opened and angels came down.

The angels taught the twelve disciples. While they were teaching, Jesus came down from heaven and began to teach the disciples.

Jesus commanded that everyone kneel down and pray. While they prayed, Jesus walked a ways off and prayed to Heavenly Father. He prayed that everyone who believed would have the Holy Ghost.

Jesus stood up and returned to where the disciples were praying. Jesus smiled when he saw them. They were filled with light and were still praying.

Jesus Christ Prophe-
sies of the Last Days

3 NEPHI 20–23, 29–30

Jesus commanded everyone to stand. He told them to continue praying in their hearts. Then Jesus made bread and wine appear. He blessed and passed it out as another sacrament for all the people.

Jesus said they were part of His chosen people, called the House of Israel. In the last days, everyone will learn about God so He can gather all of His people together.

Jesus told them that there will be a sign when this gathering begins. The sign will be when The Book of Mormon is translated and published.

The Gentiles will also learn from The Book of Mormon. Everyone not part of the House of Israel is called a Gentile. If the Gentiles repent and obey God's words, they will join the House of Israel.

In the last days, God's people will gather as part of one church. This church will be called Zion. Nothing will be able to destroy the church in the last days.

Jesus told the people that the prophet Isaiah taught about the gathering of Israel. Jesus commanded His people to study Isaiah and all the prophets.

Jesus told Nephi to go get his records. Jesus told Nephi to record one of Samuel the Lamanite's prophecies they had forgotten to write down.

Samuel had said that when Jesus appeared, many saints would rise from the dead and teach the people. So Nephi wrote Samuel's prophecy down. He also wrote many other things Jesus taught.

The Prophet Malachi's Words

3 NEPHI 24–25

Jesus told the people to write down some of the prophet Malachi's words. Heavenly Father told Malachi that He would send Elijah the prophet before the Second Coming of Jesus Christ.

Malachi wrote, "Jesus Christ will be like the fire used to make silver. The fire burns very hot until the other metals and rock burn away. Only pure silver will be left. You are that silver.

Christ will judge you for not being true to your spouse. Or for lying. Or for not paying your employees enough. Or for not taking care of the widows and fatherless children. Or for sending foreigners away.

Also, many of you have stolen from God. You stole by not paying your tithing. If you pay tithing, God will give you more blessings than you can handle.

Christ keeps a book of names. If you do and say good things, your name gets written down. That is how we will know who serves Christ and who does not.

In the final days, those who don't follow Christ will suffer. Those who do follow Christ will be protected and healed by Jesus Christ. You will know the final days are near when Elijah restores baptisms for the dead."

When Jesus was done telling them the prophet Malachi's words, He said, "God told me you did not have these scriptures. So, God commanded me to give them to you. You can now teach them to your children."

The Disciples Continue To Teach and Baptize

3 NEPHI 26

The prophet Mormon wrote that there were many more things Jesus taught the people. Mormon was going to write more, but God told him not to. God wants to test our faith with the scriptures we have.

At the day of judgment, every single person will take turns in front of God. God will judge every one of us. If we were good, then we will live forever with God. If we weren't, we won't get to live with God.

When Jesus Christ showed Himself, He taught the people for three days. He also taught and blessed the children. Babies and children taught their parents many wonderful things that cannot be written down.

Once Jesus left, the disciples began to travel. They taught and baptized as many people as they could. Everyone became members of the church.

Jesus Christ Appears Again to the Nephite Disciples

3 NEPHI 27–28

One day, the disciples were praying and fasting together. While they were praying, Jesus showed Himself to them. Jesus told them to name the church, The Church of Jesus Christ.

Jesus also taught them the gospel, "Repent and be baptized in my name. Then you will receive the Holy Ghost. The Holy Ghost will make your spirits clean. Continue to obey, and you will be saved.

Follow my example. Do the things you have seen me
do. If you do, then you will be saved. Remember this:
you will be given anything you ask Heavenly Father
for if it is good and you ask in my name.

Now write these things down. The people will be judged whether or not they follow what you write down. Everyone will be judged by the words written in the scriptures.

I am full of joy because of you and all the people choosing good. Heavenly Father and all the angels too are full of joy because of you."

Then Jesus asked, "What do you desire most from me after I return to Heavenly Father?" Nine of the disciples asked if they could return to live with Heavenly Father and Jesus in heaven after they died.

Jesus said, "You are blessed because you want this good thing. I bless you that when you die, you will return to my kingdom." Then Jesus asked the other three disciples what they wanted.

The three disciples weren't sure they should ask for what they wanted. They said nothing. Jesus said to them, "Don't be sorry for what you wish. I know your thoughts and what you want.

You wish to stay on earth and never die, so you can keep helping people repent. I bless you to never die. You will remain until I return again. You three are more blessed for wanting this."

When Jesus finished speaking, He touched the nine disciples with his finger. Then He left. The twelve received wonderful visions from heaven. They continued preaching to the people and baptizing them.

Not everyone believed the disciples. Some put the disciples into prison, but the prisons broke. Some threw them into fire, but they didn't get burned. Some put them with wild animals, but they didn't get hurt.

Anyone who believed the disciples was baptized. They became members of The Church of Jesus Christ. The disciples continued to preach the gospel of Jesus Christ.

Three Hundred Years of Nephite Righteousness

4 NEPHI

Three years had passed since Jesus Christ appeared in Bountiful. The twelve disciples preached and baptized until everyone believed and was baptized.

Everyone cared for each other. They shared all their things. There were no poor or rich. There were no prisoners or robbers. Everyone treated each other kindly and honestly.

There was peace throughout the land. The disciples continued to work miracles. They healed the sick, helped the blind to see and the deaf to hear, and raised the dead. They did all this in Jesus Christ's name.

The people rebuilt their cities. They got married and had children. They grew to be a great people. Everyone followed the gospel of Jesus Christ. They went to church, they prayed, and they fasted.

The people lived happily like this for two hundred years. Then the people began to care more about their belongings than the church. The people became more and more wicked.

After another one hundred years, almost everyone in the land was wicked. The prophet Nephi had kept the records before giving them to his son Amos.

Amos kept the records before giving them to his son, also called Amos. His son Amos kept the records until he died. Then his brother Ammaron kept the records.

Ammaron kept the records for a while. Soon the Holy Ghost told Ammaron to hide the sacred records. So Ammaron took the records and buried them in a hill.

MORMON

Mormon Is Visited by Jesus Christ

MORMON 1

Ammaron met a ten-year-old boy named Mormon. "You are a calm, thoughtful, and obedient child. When you are older, go to the hill Shim. You will find the Nephite records. Write what happens to our people."

Mormon lived in Zarahemla. In his day, the people were very wicked. But Mormon was good and steady. When he was fifteen, Jesus Christ visited him. Mormon experienced the goodness of Jesus.

Mormon tried to teach the people to repent. But the Holy Ghost made him stop. The people already knew what they were supposed to do. The people chose not to obey God and His commandments on purpose.

Mormon Commands
the Nephite Army

MORMON 2

Mormon was a large, strong boy. When he turned sixteen, the Nephites decided to make him the leader of all their armies. The Lamanites came to battle.

Mormon led the Nephite armies to fight, but they got scared. The Nephite army began to run away instead. The Lamanites chased them from the city of Angola to the land of Joshua.

The Nephites gathered in Joshua. The Lamanite king, Aaron, came and destroyed many of the Nephites. The land was also filled with robbers who stole many things. But the Nephites would not repent.

The Nephites felt sad because they couldn't sin and be happy at the same time. They were angry with God. Mormon became sad because they chose not to repent.

The Nephites ran away again to a city called Jashon. This city was near the hill where Ammaron hid the records. Mormon went and got the plates of Nephi and began to write everything happening to his people.

Again, the Nephites had to escape to a different city, which was called Shem. Here the Nephites began to beat the Lamanites in battle. Finally, the Nephites and Lamanites decided to stop fighting each other.

Mormon Preaches to the Nephites

MORMON 3

The Nephites took the land in the north. The Lamanites took the land in the south. Mormon made the Nephites prepare themselves. He knew the Lamanites would come back to fight again.

God told Mormon to tell the Nephites to repent.
Mormon tried, but the Nephites would not listen.
They had stopped caring about God.

After ten years of no fighting, the Lamanites came to battle again. The Nephites took their armies to the city called Desolation to defend themselves. Mormon helped the Nephites win.

The Nephites believed their strength helped them win—not God's help. The Nephites wanted to attack the Lamanites this time. Mormon refused. He chose not to lead the Nephite armies anymore.

The Nephites would pay for their own sins because they chose not to repent. Everyone must be judged for the good or bad they have done.

Mormon Gathers the Nephite Records

MORMON 4

The Nephites and Lamanites battled each other again and again. Sometimes the Nephites won. Sometimes the Lamanites won.

The Nephites and Lamanites were the most wicked of all God's children. Mormon learned that one way God punishes the wicked is by letting them hurt each other.

They battled for many years. Finally, the Nephites began to lose. Mormon saw that the Lamanites would soon win. So Mormon gathered up all the records Ammaron hid in the hill Shim.

The Book of Mormon Testifies of Jesus Christ

MORMON 5

The Nephites were about to all be destroyed. So Mormon decided to return and help them. But Mormon knew they would still die even with his help. They would die because they would not repent.

Mormon wrote that the stories in The Book of Mormon were to help us believe in Jesus Christ. They help us understand that Jesus Christ is Heavenly Father's Son. They help us learn the gospel of Jesus Christ.

When we stop believing in Jesus Christ, Satan has power over us. When we stop obeying the gospel, we are like a boat without a steering wheel and sail. We get tossed by the waves, unable to go anywhere.

Believe in Jesus Christ. Obey His gospel. Repent of your sins. Be humble. This means don't think you know better than God; trust in Him enough to obey Him. He will remember the prayers of those who obey.

The Battle at Cumorah
MORMON 6

Mormon wrote a letter to the king of the Lamanites. He asked the king to let the Nephites gather all the rest of their people. They would fight the Lamanites by the Hill Cumorah after the Nephites gathered.

Mormon was now an old man. He knew the Nephites would die soon. He took all the records and buried them in the Hill Cumorah. Mormon gave the last set of plates to his son Moroni.

The Nephites and Lamanites had one last battle. Over two hundred thousand Nephites died. Only Moroni and twenty-four other Nephites were still alive. Mormon was alive too, but he was wounded.

Mormon's Testimony

MORMON 7

M ormon gave his final testimony: "My people, you must no longer fight. Believe in Jesus Christ, repent of your sins, and be baptized.

Christ died and came back to life, so we can too. Our spirits and bodies will come back together. We will stand in front of God. He will judge us for all the good and bad we did. Follow the gospel of Jesus Christ.

Repent, be baptized, and receive the Holy Ghost. If you obey this gospel, you can enter God's kingdom. To have the Holy Ghost be with you, you must obey and live God's commandments."

Moroni Gets the Plates

MORMON 8

Moroni wrote on the plates. He said after the great battle on the Hill Cumorah, the Lamanites found and killed Mormon.

Moroni was now the last Nephite alive. The land was filled with Lamanites and robbers. They fought with each other.

Moroni would finish writing on the plates and bury them. He said one day God would let the plates be found. The words written on the plates would be shared with the whole earth.

The world will be a wicked place when the plates are found. People will no longer believe in or follow God. They will build churches to make money for themselves.

Moroni Writes to Us in the Latter Days

MORMON 9

Moroni wrote to us who live in the latter days. He said, "I speak to those who do not believe in Jesus Christ. Pray to God in Jesus Christ's name.

If you do not believe in miracles or revelations, then you don't understand the scriptures. The scriptures teach that God does not change. He will always be a God of miracles and revelation.

God created the heavens and the earth. God created Adam and Eve. Because of them, all people on earth are alive. Because of them, they can also sin. So God sent Jesus Christ to save us all from sin.

Because of Jesus Christ we can all live again after we die. When we are resurrected, we will return to God. God will judge us. If we are good and clean, we will be happy."

ETHER

God Doesn't Change the Jaredite Language

ETHER 1

King Limhi's people had found the Jaredite records on twenty-four plates. The Jaredite records told the stories of the creation and Adam and Eve. It had many stories written up through the Tower of Babel.

The Jaredite record was written by the prophet Ether. Ether was a descendant of Jared. Jared lived at the time the people built the Tower of Babel, when God changed everyone's language.

The brother of Jared was called Mahonri Moriancumer. Mahonri was a large and mighty man. God loved Mahonri very much. Jared asked Mahonri to pray to God: "Ask Him to not change our language."

Mahonri prayed that God would not change the language of his family or friends. God heard his prayer and didn't change their language. Mahonri also asked if they should leave and go somewhere else.

God told Mahonri to gather his family and their friends. God commanded them to pack their things and move to a valley north of the city. From here, God would lead them to a promised land.

The Jaredites Travel and Build Boats
ETHER 2

M ahonri and Jared's people gathered things for their journey. They brought all their animals. They even brought fish, bees, and seeds. Then they went up to the valley Nimrod that God had revealed to them.

When they arrived, God came down in a cloud and spoke with Mahonri, the brother of Jared. Mahonri couldn't see God, but he could hear Him. God commanded Mahonri to lead the people into the desert.

So the families obeyed. God continued to help them while they traveled. God directed them where to go. He would continue leading them to the promised land.

God told Mahonri that He had blessed the promised land. If the people obeyed God, then they would be blessed. If they didn't obey God, they would be destroyed.

After many days, the people called the Jaredites arrived at the ocean. They pitched their tents. They called the seashore Moriancumer. They stayed for four years before God spoke with Mahonri again.

God was not happy with Mahonri, the brother of Jared, because he had forgotten to pray. Mahonri repented. God forgave him. God warned him to keep praying, or else the Spirit could not guide him.

God showed Mahonri how to build special boats. God commanded the Jaredites to build them. The boats were small, lightweight, and tight like a dish. They were closed so tight that air and light could not get into the boat.

When the Jaredites finished, Mahonri prayed to God. "God, we have finished building eight boats like you have shown us. But they are so tight that we cannot see or breathe in them. We will die in them."

God told Mahonri, the brother of Jared, to cut a small hole in the top and bottom of each boat. If the Jaredites needed air, they could pull out a plug to breathe. Mahonri obeyed and cut holes in the boats.

Mahonri prayed again, "God, we obeyed and cut holes in the boats. But there is still no light in them. Do you wish us to travel in the dark?" God answered, "What should I do so that you have light in the boats?

Windows will break, and you can't have fire in the boats. These boats will travel like whales under the water. Waves and wind will push you toward the promised land. So tell me what you would like me to do."

Mahonri Sees Jesus Christ

ETHER 3

Mahonri, the brother of Jared, went up the mountain Shelem. There he melted a rock into sixteen small stones. The stones were clear as glass. He took them to the top of the mountain and prayed to God.

God, You gave us a commandment to pray to You if we need something. Please don't let us travel in darkness. I know if You touch these small stones, they will shine light in the boats."

Jesus Christ reached down and touched each stone with His finger to make them shine. Mahonri saw Christ's finger. He fell onto the ground afraid. Jesus said, "Stand. Why did you fall?"

"I saw Your finger. I didn't know You had a body of flesh and blood." Jesus replied, "Because of your faith, you were able to see me. Did you see more than my finger?" "No," said Mahonri. "Show Yourself to me."

"Will you believe my words?" asked Jesus. "I know You will only tell the truth," said Mahonri. So Jesus showed Himself to Mahonri. "You are saved. Because of your great faith, you can see me," said Jesus.

"I am Jesus Christ. I will save whoever believes in me. No one has believed in me as much as you have. Do you see how your body was made like my body? This is my spirit body now. Later, I will have a body of flesh.

Now, Mahonri, do not tell anyone what you saw and heard today. Just write it down." He then gave two stones to Mahonri and said, "One day, I will let others read your record using these two stones."

Then Jesus showed Mahonri the history of the earth, from the beginning to the end. "Write down everything I have shown you. Hide the record and the stones together. One day, everyone will read your record."

Moroni Adds the Jaredite Records to the Gold Plates

ETHER 4–5

Moroni took what Mahonri, the brother of Jared, had written and copied it to the Gold Plates. God commanded Moroni to seal and hide them with the two stone interpreters Jesus gave Mahonri.

Mahonri's records won't be shared until the non-believers repent and have faith. Then Jesus Christ will explain His revelations. Moroni wrote that those who don't believe won't be shown anything else.

Those who believe will receive the Spirit and know that the records are true. They will know the records are true because they teach us to do good. Anything that leads you to do good comes from Jesus Christ.

Christ said, "Come to me, and I will give you knowledge. Repent, believe my gospel, and be baptized. Then you will be saved. Whoever follows my commandments until the end will live with me in heaven."

Moroni explained that the Gold Plates would be shown to three witnesses. These three witnesses would share their testimony that The Book of Mormon is true.

The Jaredites Multiply and Choose a King

ETHER 6

Mahonri took the two stone interpreters and the sixteen stones that Christ touched. He walked back down the mountain. He put two stones in each boat for light while they traveled across the ocean.

The people prepared food, water, and their animals. They got into the boats and set off. God created a great wind that began to push the boats. The wind never stopped blowing them toward the promised land.

The boats often went under the water, but they didn't leak. Whales couldn't harm them. Mahonri and his people praised God. They traveled for three hundred forty-four days before arriving at the promised land.

They landed on shore and thanked God for blessing them. The Jaredites began to build and farm on the land. Altogether, there were twenty-two Jaredites who traveled across the ocean.

Soon the Jaredites began to have many children. They were all taught to follow God and His commandments. They grew to become a strong and humble people.

When Mahonri and Jared grew old, they gathered their families. They asked their families if they wanted anything before they died. They asked for Mahonri and Jared to choose someone to be their king.

This made Mahonri and Jared worried. They knew kings weren't always good. But they let the people choose a king. Each of Mahonri and Jared's sons refused to be king except for Jared's son Orihah.

Orihah became their king. He was a good and humble king who taught his people to follow God. The people soon grew very rich. After some time, Jared and Mahonri grew old and died.

The Jaredites Begin To Fight Each Other

ETHER 7

Orihah lived a long time and had many children. He had thirty-one children. One of his sons was named Kib. Orihah made Kib the king. Kib had many children too. One of Kib's sons was called Corihor.

Corihor was not a good person. He didn't like obeying his father. He ran away to a place called Nehor. While in Nehor, Corihor had many children. His daughters were beautiful, and his sons were handsome.

Corihor's children got others to leave Kib's kingdom. When enough people had left the kingdom, Corihor led them back and took over the city. He put his father, Kib, in prison.

While Kib was in prison, he had another son named Shule. Shule grew up to be a very strong and wise man. Now Shule was angry with Corihor for what he did to their father, Kib.

Shule and others escaped from Corihor. Shule went to a hill called Ephraim and made swords for everyone who had escaped. They took their swords and went back to the city to fight Corihor.

Shule freed his father, Kib, from prison. Kib made Shule king over the people. Corihor felt very sorry for everything he had done. Shule saw his brother was sorry, so he let Corihor help him rule the kingdom.

One of Corihor's sons was named Noah. Noah was angry with his uncle Shule and his father, Corihor. So Noah got his brother and many of the people to fight against Shule.

Noah and his army took over part of the land. The people who followed Noah made him their king in that part of the land. Noah also captured Shule and put him in prison.

Noah planned to kill Shule. Before he could, Shule's sons snuck into Noah's house and killed him first. Shule's sons broke down the prison door and helped their father escape.

Noah's son Cohor became king. Cohor fought against Shule but was killed in battle. Nimrod, Cohor's son, gave the kingdom back to Shule. Shule was so thankful that he gave Nimrod many gifts.

While Shule was king, the people began to disobey God's commandments. So God called prophets to help the people repent. The prophets told the Jaredites they would be destroyed if they did not repent.

Many of the Jaredites made fun of the prophets. They argued with the prophets. When King Shule saw this, he made a law. The law let the prophets teach wherever they wanted to in his kingdom.

Because of Shule's law and the prophets' teachings, the people finally repented. Because the people repented, God did not destroy them. Again the Jaredites were blessed and began to be very rich.

Shule began to be old. He was a good king who followed God's commandments. He always reminded himself of God's goodness for leading the Jaredites across the ocean.

Akish and the Secret Society

ETHER 8

Shule had a son named Omer who became king. Omer's son Jared was disobedient. Jared decided to leave the kingdom to go to a place called Heth. There he began to build an army.

Once Jared had an army, he took over the kingdom and locked his father in prison. Jared's brothers Esrom and Coriantumr fought back and beat him. When Jared lost the kingdom, it made him very sad.

Jared's daughter was very beautiful and smart. She didn't like seeing her father so sad. She made a plan. She told her father to invite over a man named Akish. When Akish came, Jared's daughter danced for him.

Akish asked Jared if he could marry his daughter. Jared said, "I will let you marry her, if you kill my father, King Omer." Omer and Akish were friends, but Akish agreed to Jared's plan because he wanted power.

Akish called his family and friends together. They promised to help Akish and to keep it a secret. They created a secret society—a secret group that does evil things. These secret groups come from Satan.

Moroni warned us to be careful of these secret societies. Any country with secret societies will be destroyed. Secret societies don't care about anyone's freedom. They only want power and money.

The Jaredites Nearly Destroy Themselves

ETHER 9

A kish and his secret society made plans to kill King Omer. But God warned Omer in a dream. So Omer took his family and left the city. They traveled far away to a place by the sea called Ablom.

Jared became king, and he gave Akish his daughter to marry for helping him. But Akish wanted to be king. So Akish got his secret society together. They killed Jared and made Akish king.

One of Akish's sons did not like what his father was doing. He took some of his friends and they left to live with Omer and his family. Akish's other sons were like Akish. They only cared about power and money.

Soon, Akish and his sons began to battle each other. Everyone in the city either fought for Akish or one of his sons. They fought for many years. Finally, everyone in the city was destroyed, except for thirty people.

Omer and his family returned. Omer was very old, so he made his son Emer the king. King Emer was a good king who followed God. Emer's people grew wealthy and had peace for sixty-two years.

Emer made his son Coriantum king. Coriantum was a good king. And Coriantum's son Com was also a good king. But Com's son Heth was not a good man. Heth had his secret society make him king.

God saw that the Jaredites were beginning to be wicked. So God sent prophets to tell the people to repent or be destroyed. The people did not listen. They threw the prophets out of their cities.

The Jaredites would not repent, so God did not let it rain. Without rain, no food could grow. God also sent snakes to scare their animals away. The Jaredites began to starve without anything to eat or drink.

Once the Jaredites saw they were about to die, they began to repent. They prayed for forgiveness. When they had repented enough, God sent them rain. And food began to grow again.

Wicked Kings Lead to Destruction

ETHER 10–11

H eth's son Shez began to rebuild the kingdom and his people. Shez was a good king who followed God's commandments. When Shez grew old, he gave the kingdom to his son Riplakish.

Riplakish did not follow God's commandments. Riplakish decided to marry many women. He also taxed the people a lot. He used the tax money to build large, beautiful buildings.

If the people couldn't pay their taxes, he put them into prison. In prison, he forced the people to make nice things for his buildings. After many years, the people killed Riplakish and forced his family to run away.

Riplakish's son Morianton gathered an army and took back the kingdom. He lowered their taxes and was a good king to the people. But Morianton did not obey God's commandments in his own life.

The Jaredites had many kings. Some kings were good and followed God's commandments. Other kings were not good and caused the people to sin. The Jaredites worked hard, so they had many nice things.

Whenever the people began to be wicked, God would send prophets. The prophets would warn the people to repent or be destroyed. Sometimes the people listened and were saved. Other times the people did not listen, so many of them were destroyed.

Faith, Hope, and Grace

ETHER 12

After many years, there was a king named Coriantumr. God sent a prophet to Coriantumr and his people. This prophet was called Ether.

Ether was a great prophet. He tried to warn the people they would be destroyed if they did not believe in God and repent. Ether warned the people from sunrise to sunset.

Ether taught the people many great and wonderful things, but the people did not believe him. They didn't believe because they couldn't see Ether's prophecies.

Moroni explained that trusting and believing in something you cannot see yet is called faith. Faith leads us to act even though we cannot see what will happen next.

If we have faith in Jesus Christ, it means we believe in Him enough to do the things He has taught, even if we don't know why. God can do many things for us if we just have faith.

There have been many things that were done through faith. Mahonri, the brother of Jared, believed in Jesus Christ so much that he saw Christ's finger touch the stones.

Because of Alma and Amulek's faith, they broke free of the ropes they were tied with. Because of their faith, the prison they were in crumbled to the earth, and they were not hurt.

Because of Nephi and Lehi's faith, thousands of Lamanites repented and were baptized. Because of their faith, a pillar of fire surrounded them in prison to show God's power to the Lamanites.

Because of Ammon and his brothers' faith, many Lamanites came to know the truth. Because of their faith, they had the spirit of prophecy and revelation. They had been given great power and authority from God.

The three Nephite disciples showed faith too. Because of their faith, they received a promise that they would never die. Miracles only happen when someone first believes in God and acts in faith.

Mahonri's faith was so strong, he said, "Move!" to a mountain, and it moved! Faith is important, but we must also be humble. Being humble means you trust God more than you trust anyone else, including yourself.

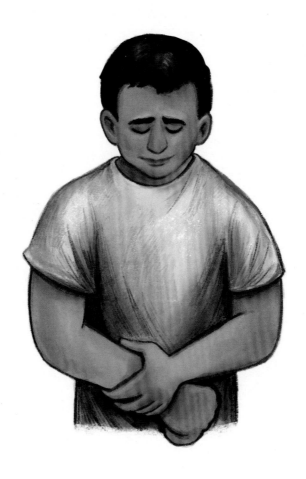

When we are humble, we care more about what God cares about. We care less about what the world cares about. We don't think we are better than other people.

If we are humble and choose to do whatever God wants, then God will show us our weakness. God gives everyone weakness so we may learn to trust Him.

If we are humble and have faith in Jesus Christ, then He will give us strength, called grace. He will help us do good things we could not do without His help.

The Prophet Ether Warns King Coriantumr

ETHER 13

Ether taught the Jaredites about many great and important things. But the people did not believe him. They threw him out of the city.

Ether had to hide in a cave. At night, Ether would come out of the cave and watch what happened to the people. He would write down everything he saw happening.

Ether watched as a great war broke out among Coriantumr's people. There were many strong men who tried to take the kingdom away from Coriantumr. But Coriantumr was strong and fought against them.

God told Ether to go give Coriantumr a message. Ether obeyed. He told Coriantumr that if he and his family repented, God would let Coriantumr keep his kingdom. God would also save all the Jaredites.

If Coriantumr and his family did not repent, all the Jaredites would be destroyed. God would let Coriantumr live long enough to watch everyone die. He would see the Nephites take over the land. Then he would die.

Coriantumr and his family did not repent. They tried to kill Ether. Ether ran away and hid in his cave. Coriantumr continued his war against everyone who tried to take his kingdom away.

Now there was another man named Shared who fought against Coriantumr. They battled against each other many times until Coriantumr finally beat and killed Shared.

Coriantumr Fights Gilead,
Lib, Then Shiz

ETHER 14

A curse fell over the land. If the people didn't hold onto their things, their things would disappear. They always had to carry their swords with them to defend themselves.

Shared's brother Gilead was angry with Coriantumr. Gilead fought Coriantumr. Gilead attacked Coriantumr's men at night while they were drunk. He won and took over the kingdom.

For two years, Coriantumr stayed in the wilderness and built up his army. Gilead continued to rule the kingdom. But there was a secret society that killed Gilead and made another man king. His name was Lib.

Coriantumr battled King Lib. When Lib died, his brother became king. His name was Shiz. Shiz was a very strong man who fought very hard. He fought Coriantumr and chased his people for many days.

Shiz and Coriantumr's armies fought against each other for many days. One day, while they were fighting, Shiz wounded Coriantumr so badly that Coriantumr fainted. Everyone thought he was dead.

The Jaredites Completely Destroy Themselves

ETHER 15

Coriantumr was not dead. He healed from his wounds. While he was healing, he remembered Ether's words. Coriantumr would live long enough to watch all his people die. Two million people had already died.

Coriantumr began to repent. He wanted his people to live. So Coriantumr wrote a letter to Shiz asking him for peace. But Shiz and his people were angry with Coriantumr. Instead, they came to battle him again.

So Coriantumr and his army battled Shiz and his army. They battled again and again. Ether watched as all the Jaredites fought each other. Everyone fought for either Shiz or Coriantumr.

The Jaredites gathered for battle near the Hill Cumorah. Both armies made every man, woman, and child wear armor and fight in the battle. They fought all day long, but no one won.

Coriantumr sent another letter to Shiz asking for peace, but Shiz refused. So both armies fought day after day. Finally, Shiz only had thirty-two people left. Coriantumr only had twenty-seven people left.

On the last day of fighting, everyone died except for Coriantumr and Shiz. Shiz was wounded and fainted. Coriantumr rested for a while on his sword. Then Coriantumr killed Shiz and fainted too.

Ether finished his record. He took his records and hid them where they could be found by the Nephites. Ether's final words said, "It doesn't matter what happens to me now, as long as I am saved in God's kingdom. Amen."

MORONI

Laying on of Hands, Ordaining, and the Sacrament

MORONI 1–5

Moroni hid from the Lamanites. He wrote a few more things down on the plates. He wanted to share more about what Jesus said and did when He came and visited the Nephites.

Jesus Christ told His twelve Nephite disciples to pray to God in Christ's name. They had the power to give the gift of the Holy Ghost to others. The disciples did this by laying their hands on the person's head.

The disciples ordained priests and teachers. Ordain means to bless someone and invite them to help God. The priests and teachers taught the people to have faith in Jesus Christ and repent of their sins.

Jesus showed the disciples how to bless the sacrament. The sacrament helps us remember Jesus Christ's Atonement. When we take the sacrament, we promise to remember Jesus Christ and keep His commandments.

Being Members of The Church of Jesus Christ

MORONI 6

Jesus Christ taught about baptism. We're ready for baptism when we feel sorry for things we have done wrong, trust God enough to obey His commandments, and have changed how we think and act.

When we are baptized, we promise to be an example of Jesus Christ, the power of the Holy Ghost cleans away our sins, and we become a member of The Church of Jesus Christ.

The members of the church write down our names when we're baptized, so we don't forget each other. We help each other. We teach each other the words of God. We pray together and follow Jesus Christ.

As members of the church, we meet together often to fast and to pray. We teach each other how to return to God. We meet to have the sacrament and show we remember Jesus Christ and our promises to Him.

In all of our meetings, we follow the Spirit. The power of the Holy Ghost will help us know when to teach, pray, ask for forgiveness, repent, or sing.

Mormon Teaches about Faith, Hope, and Charity

MORONI 7

Moroni shared one of his father's talks from church. Mormon said in his talk, "Watch what people do. If they do good things, then they are also good people.

All good things come from God. Everything else comes from Satan. God gave us the Spirit to help us know when something is good or not. If you choose to do good things, then you will have the Spirit.

Angels and prophets have said Jesus Christ will come. Believe in Jesus and trust Him—this is called faith. Believe God will answer your prayers. If you pray to God in Jesus Christ's name with faith, He will answer you.

God's angels show themselves to anyone who has strong faith. Angels always teach of Jesus Christ. They teach us to repent and keep our promises with God. These promises are called covenants.

Jesus tells us to repent and be baptized. If we do, we can be saved. Being saved is called salvation. Salvation means we get to live with God again in heaven.

When we have hope, we are sure God will keep His promises to us. We can hope for salvation because of Jesus Christ's Atonement and resurrection. Jesus Christ's experience suffering in the Garden of Gethsemane and on the cross is called the Atonement.

Having faith and hope in Jesus Christ will make us happy, calm, and courageous. We must also love others the way God does. This kind of love is called charity. You know you have charity when you are calm and kind to others.

You have charity when you care about everyone, even people who are hard to love. This is how Jesus Christ loves everyone. If we try to love like Him, we cannot fail. We are nothing if we don't try to love as He does. So pray to God that you will always have this love."

Mormon Teaches about Baptism
MORONI 8

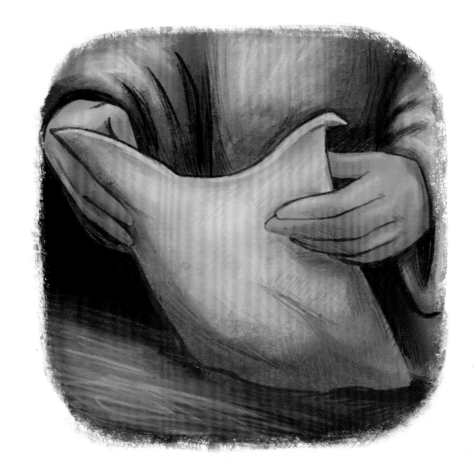

Mormon wrote Moroni a letter when Moroni started serving in the church. Mormon wrote the letter because the Nephites Moroni was teaching wanted to baptize their little children.

Mormon wrote, "I prayed to God to know the truth. God sent the Holy Ghost who told me little children cannot sin. Only people who can sin need to repent and be baptized. Little children are saved by Jesus Christ.

Those who don't know God's laws are also saved by Jesus. You have to know you broke God's law before you can repent. So they are not punished. The first sign that you have repented is baptism.

When you have faith in Jesus Christ, you will want to be baptized. After baptism, God forgives your sins when you obey His commandments. When God forgives you, you will feel calm and confident. The Holy Ghost will fill you with hope and charity."

The Nephites and Lamanites Are Wicked

MORONI 9

In another letter, Mormon wrote, "I am worried the Lamanites will destroy the Nephites. The Nephites don't repent. They are always angry with each other. I am still trying to teach them to choose the right.

When I teach them what God has said, the Nephites either get angry with me or they don't listen. I worry the Spirit can no longer help them. They don't care about anything anymore, not even their own lives.

Even though they won't listen, Moroni, we must still teach them. God commanded us to teach while we are still alive. If we do, we will live with God in His kingdom again.

The Lamanites have taken many men, women, and children as prisoners. They kill the men. So the widows, daughters, and old women are left to suffer. But the Nephites do even worse things to the Lamanites!

Moroni, I know I will see you soon. I have the Gold Plates that I need to give to you. Have faith in Jesus Christ. Have hope that we will someday live forever in heaven with God. Amen."

Moroni's Final Testimony

MORONI 10

"I, Moroni, ask that when you read The Book of Mormon, remember how kind and patient God has been to all His children. Think about His kindness, and feel it in your heart. Pray when you get the scriptures.

Ask God in Jesus Christ's name if the scriptures are not true. Make sure you want to know the truth. Be willing to change your life if they are true. Believe in Jesus Christ. Then God will tell you the record is true with the Holy Ghost.

The Holy Ghost has power. His power can help us know all true things. All good things are true. All good things show that Jesus Christ lives. The power of the Holy Ghost will help you know that Jesus Christ is real.

God gives us special gifts through the Spirit to help us. Some have the gift of faith or the gift of healing or the gift of teaching. There are many gifts God can give us. He will always give us gifts, unless we stop believing in Him.

Come to Christ. If you are good and love God, He will help you become perfect. As God helps you become perfect, you will be blessed and cleansed from sin. I will meet you after this life when Jesus Christ comes to judge us all. Amen.

About the Author and Illustrator

AUTHOR

Jason Zippro holds a master's degree in education from the University of Missouri-Saint Louis, a master's degree in business administration from the University of Utah, and a bachelor of arts degree in Italian with a minor in editing from Brigham Young University. Jason worked as an editor for four years before teaching 8th grade English for three years in Kansas City with the non-profit Teach for America. Jason and his wife, Sharolee, have four young children.

ILLUSTRATOR

Alycia Pace graduated from Brigham Young University with a bachelor of fine arts degree in animation and is a freelance illustrator from her home in Utah. She has written and illustrated several books including *Polly the Perfectly Polite Pig* (available at Deseret Book and Barnes & Noble) and soon to be available, *How to Train a Dinosaur to Use the Potty*. She loves the smell of bookstores and exploring new places with her two children and adventurous husband.